Centre for Reformation and Renaissance Studies
University of Toronto

Translation Series 3

BERNARDINO OCHINO

Seven Dialogues

Translated, with an introduction and notes, by
RITA BELLADONNA

DOVEHOUSE EDITIONS
CANADA
1988

Canadian Cataloguing in Publication Data

Ochino, Bernardino, 1487-1564
    Seven dialogues = I dialogi sette

(Renaissance and Reformation texts in translation ; 3)
Translation of: I dialogi sette.
Bibliography: p.
ISBN 0-919473-63-6

1. Dialogues, Italian—Translations into
English. 2. Dialogues, English—Translations
from Italian. 3. Christian Life.
4. Devotional literature. I. Belladonna, Rita
II. Title. III. Title: I dialogi sette.
IV. Series.

BR350.03D4313 1987   248   C87-090300-4

For information on distribution and for placing orders:
        Dovehouse Editions, Canada
        32 Glen Ave.
        Ottawa, Canada
        K1S 2Z7

For further information about the series:
        The Editors, Renaissance and Reformation texts in trans-
        lation
        Centre for Reformation and Renaissance Studies
        Victoria University in the University of Toronto
        71 Queen's Park Crescent
        Toronto, Canada, M5S 1K7

CONTENTS

Acknowledgements   vi

Introduction   vii

Editorial Note   xxx

Notes to the Introduction   xxxiii

Select Bibliography   xlii

A Dialogue About How to Grow to Love God   1

A Dialogue About How to Achieve Happiness   21

A Dialogue About How a Man Should
    Best Govern Himself   27

A Dialogue About the Thief on the Cross   43

A Dialogue About the Need to be Converted Early   51

A Dialogue About the Pilgrimage to Heaven   59

A Dialogue About the Divine Profession of Faith   71

Notes to the Dialogues   83

ACKNOWLEDGEMENTS

Publication of this book has been made possible by a generous grant from the Faculty of Arts, York University for which I am extremely grateful.

Thanks are due to the Reverend Father V. van Zutphen of St. Peter's Seminary, London, Ontario, for his patient help in supplying many indispensable theological explanations. Professor Joan Lenardon read the text and notes supplying excellent comments and suggestions.

Finally, very special thanks are due to Margaret Bukta who repeatedly revised the text spotting numerous errors and suggested many invaluable improvements.

INTRODUCTION

Bernardino Ochino's writings, like his life, are sharply divided by his escape from Italy in the late summer of 1542. His production before that date consists of two collections of *Sermones* (sermons) and the *Dialogi Sette* (seven dialogues). Whereas the texts of the sermons are only partial transcriptions of what the original versions must have been, the *Dialogi* no doubt constitute a more complete expression of Ochino's thought. The tantalizing ambiguity of their religious content has been noted by various critics. For example, according to Cuthbert of Brighton, were it not for the author's escape to the Protestant world the *Dialogi* could be viewed as an expression of the Catholic reform.[1] Roland Bainton remarks on the derivation from St. Bonaventure.[2] At least two critics in years past have remarked on the affinities between the *Dialogi* and some aspects of Protestant thought.[3] It would appear, therefore, that the *Dialogi Sette* share in the fluctuating ambiguity of Italian Evangelism.

LIFE

Bernardino Ochino, whose family name was Tommasini, was born in Siena around 1487. The nickname Ochino originated from the fact that he was born in the *Contrada dell'Oca* (goose), one of the seventeen *contrade* or quarters into which Siena is still divided. His father, Domenico, was a barber by profession, however, nothing else is known about Ochino's family or childhood. In 1503 or 1504 he decided to join the Franciscan Friars Observant at Capriola, a monastery one mile from Siena, taking the name of Saint Bernardino, the Sienese Franciscan saint.[4] The Friars Observant came into existence at the end of the fourteenth century as a reaction against the laxity pervading the Franciscan Order. Over time the Franciscans had strayed farther and farther away from the original Rule of St. Francis. The original core Order continued to exist and had come to be known as the Friars Conventual.

Introduction

At Capriola Ochino studied Latin, Greek, and Hebrew, as well as the works of St. Bonaventure, St. Thomas Aquinas, Duns Scotus, Plato, Aristotle and others. In 1510 he temporarily left the monastery to obtain a doctorate in medicine at Perugia University. Among his fellow-students was Cardinal Giulio de' Medici, the future Pope Clement VII. Upon Ochino's return to Capriola he resumed his theological studies with renewed interest. His superiors must have appreciated him since, when the Franciscan Tuscan Province became divided into the Province of Florence and that of Siena in 1523, Ochino was elected to be the first Provincial of the latter. Tension quickly developed between the Florentine Province and the newly-created Sienese one. In 1526 Ochino obtained for the Sienese friars the right to be called the Tuscan Province proper, whereas the Florentine friars were only entitled to be called the Tuscan Florentine Province.[5] Even as a Franciscan, Ochino still took pride in his Sienese origins.

In the spring of 1530 Ochino was entrusted with a delicate task by his superior, Paolo Pisotti of Parma. Already in 1529, the friars in the Venetian Province had been severely divided into factions over the election of their Provincial. Three friars each wished to be elected. Pisotti, who was a corrupt man, had arranged for one of the friars to be elected. The understanding was that he would leave the post vacant one year later to make room for one of the other two friars, both more favoured by Pisotti. Ochino was to preside over the preconcerted election.

The friar refused to give up his position as promised. Ochino was sent to Mantua in June to persuade him to follow the original agreement. Despite the opposition of all the friars of the Venetian Province, an accord was reached to hold a general meeting in autumn. Ochino returned to Capriola only to receive the news that Clement pressed for an immediate meeting, and he was sent back in compliance with the Pope's instructions. His presence, however, awakened such resentment on the part of the Venetian friars, that Ochino had to ask Gianpietro Carafa, the future Pope Paul IV, to intervene in his favour. A meeting was called on September 13, 1531, and presided over by Ochino.

In the meantime, Clement had second thoughts. After Ochino left Capriola, the Pope sent two briefs to Gian Matteo Giberti, Bishop of Verona. In one of them he prorogued the meeting to November; in the other he instructed Giberti to appoint a friar to investigate the situation in the Venetian Province. That information was to be studied by Carafa, who was to suggest ways of correcting the obvious abuses that abounded in that part of the Order. Clement intimated that he would have preferred the information to be gathered by Ochino; however, Giberti disliked Ochino and appointed another friar to conduct the inquiry. All that was left for Ochino to do was to call an official end to the September meeting and to return to Capriola. After closing the meeting he wrote to Carafa expressing his regret that the papal briefs had not arrived earlier.[6] This was probably a veiled expression of his own frustration at the petty rivalries and intrigues of an Order in which he had expected to find spiritual perfection. Carafa himself reported to Clement in 1532 that the majority of corrupt friars oppressed the good ones to such an extent that they rendered any attempt at reform impossible.[7] In the midst of such mundane controversies Ochino must have felt more than once that he was losing sight of his original pursuit, a life devoted to God and to his fellow-beings.

It is quite probable that during the years when he was involved in the problems of the Venetian Province, Ochino made the acquaintance of Agostino Mainardi, Giulio della Rovere and Pietro Martire Vermigli; — all members of other religious orders who had more or less secret sympathies toward Protestantism. Though it is hard to pinpoint such events, Ochino's friendship with them and his more direct exposure to Protestant thought may antedate his own escape in 1542 by as much as ten years.[8]

Meanwhile, in the early 1520's a renewed current of asceticism developed within the Franciscan Order. Led by Matteo da Bascio, it emphasized a return to the original Franciscan ideals of poverty and contemplation, based on the imitation of Christ.[9] His desire for reform, however, awakened the opposition of the other Franciscans, who were not pleased at the prospect of a split in the Order and perhaps also feared the revival of the heretical tendencies which had already appeared among the Franciscans in previous centuries.[10] Matteo da Bascio was temporarily imprisoned in 1525 by Giovanni da Fano, a Franciscan Provincial.

Matteo da Bascio had fortunately gained the admiration of Caterina Cybo, the young and energetic Duchess of Camerino, who was also Clement VII's second cousin. It was largely thanks to her help that, eventually in 1528, the new group obtained official recognition. Members of this Order came to be known as *Cappuccini* (Capuchins) because of the shape of their hoods (*cappucci*) which, they claimed, was similar to that of the hood of St. Francis. The austerity required of the Capuchins is reflected in their revised Constitution, written in Rome in 1536. They had to live in ascetic isolation from the world and to follow the original Rule of St. Francis, which included total poverty; flagellation was a regular practice in commemoration of Christ's Passion.[11]

In 1534 Ochino became a Capuchin, even though he had been elected Definitor General of the Observants in 1532.[12] His preaching and personality had already attracted the attention of his contemporaries. Now his ascetic lifestyle became obvious. It was increasingly noticed that he travelled on foot regardless of the weather, and that during his frequent journeys as an itinerant preacher he often slept on the ground under a tree. He had become so well known that people sometimes knelt when they met him and asked for his blessing. He never ate meat, he sat at a table only once a day, and his meals consisted of only one simple dish.[13] His fame as a preacher, while he was still among the Observants and especially after he joined the Capuchins, spread far and wide. He was praised and admired by, among others, Vittoria Colonna, Pietro Bembo, Giovanni Guidiccioni, and Tullia d'Aragona. In a letter to Giustiniano Nelli written from Venice on March 20, 1539, Pietro Aretino described Ochino's preaching in these years as follows:

> "God has bestowed on him the great gift of expressing his thoughts, explaining Scripture and rebuking vice. With his well-meaning warnings and his terrible threats he touches and fright-

ens people; thus he inspires them to hope and repent. Every mind and every heart is moved and held in check when Ochino's eyes and words probe into people's thoughts and intentions. The fervour of his preaching and the way his lofty sincere tone is sustained throughout are incredible. I venture to say that no one has preached like him since the times of the Apostles. The pure original meaning of St. Paul resounds in his exclamations, so appropriately formed and inserted and so appropriately interrupted. How brightly shines the Gospel when interwoven with the Christian meaning of his own personal remarks! With what lucid and lively links he binds the Old and New Testaments together, always keeping their sacred meaning within the boundaries of true religion! Therefore, crowds flock to listen to him as if he were the Baptist in the wilderness. The meaning full of wit and the wit full of meaning, which may be seen and heard in the Catholicism of his sermons, are superhuman. The weighty body of his preaching breathes with such power and vehemence that one can clearly see how nature and knowledge both prompt him to proclaim things pertaining to the true, almighty, and only God. Truly he is the honour of his Order and of our Italy. One cannot but marvel at his ways, for he has a forceful eloquence, a graceful elocution, a profound knowledge, a refined language, a resounding voice, an astounding fame, a majestic presence, the nobility of his mother-country, a praiseworthy life, the wisdom of age, and a sincere spirit. Moreover, all that he says relates to mercy, salvation, and the remission of sins."[14]

Ochino's career as a Capuchin was as outwardly successful as his career among the Observants. In 1534, just after being admitted to the new Order, he preached at S. Lorenzo in Damaso in Rome. He was heard on that occasion by Pietro Carnesecchi, who several years later was charged with heresy and executed, and possibly also by Juan de Valdés, who at that time still lived in Rome.[15] In 1535 Ludovico da Fossombrone, the autocratic General of the Capuchins, was replaced by Bernardino d'Asti and Ochino was elected First Definitor of the Order. Together with Bernardino d'Asti he contributed to the 1536 revision of the Capuchin Constitution.

By now, Ochino seemed to many people to be the living incarnation of the ideals of St. Francis. A description dating to some years later, by an observer who was biased against him, follows:

> "Everything about Ochino contributed to make the admiration of the multitude overstep all human bounds . . .; his prepossessing, ingratiating manner; his advancing years; his mode of life; the rough Capucin garb; the long beard reaching to his breast; the grey hair; the pale, thin face; the artificially induced aspect of bodily weakness; finally, the reputation of a holy life. Wherever he was to speak the citizens could be seen in crowds; no church was large enough to contain the multitude of listeners."[16]

In 1538 Ochino was elected General of the Capuchins replacing Bernardino d'Asti who had been gravely ill.

Yet, in spite of Ochino's external success, his conscience must have been troubled by doubts. As already seen, some of his oldest friends in other religious orders appeared to show signs of leaning toward Protestantism. An important event in his life, his meeting with Juan de Valdés, took place during Lent, 1536, when Ochino preached in S. Giovanni Maggiore in Naples. The Spanish thinker had moved to that city in 1534, after Clement VII's death. Valdés' life had developed along the paths of piety, humanistic learning and papal-imperial diplomacy.[17] Starting as a follower of Erasmus, he had developed his own original religious thought in a way which, at times, brought him very close to some aspects of Protestantism. Following Erasmus' tendency to devalue whatever was external in religion, Valdés emphasized the subjective inner experience of faith.[18] Thus it became essential for the believer to experience faith as a living force, as opposed to mechanically following what was prescribed by the Church.[19] The direct experience of faith, accompanied by the cathartic contemplation of Christ's sacrifice on the Cross, would necessarily result in good works. Valdés considered works totally useless unless they were preceded and prompted by living faith. Justification by faith became the basis of his thought. However, it is important to realise that he never pursued his teaching to the point of advocating a radical reform of the Church.[20] Instead he stressed the importance of the inner reform of the individual. This is evident in his *Alfabeto Cristiano*, written in 1536, in which Valdés depicted himself in conversation with Julia Gonzaga, who was reacting to the impact of Ochino's preaching in Naples. She formed part of the learned aristocratic circle among whose members Valdés' ideas were first discussed, before spreading to other parts of Italy.[21]

Valdés' religious thought was of enormous importance in Ochino's spiritual development. Ochino's friendship with several individuals who inclined toward Protestantism had already prepared his mind for the reception of untraditional religious ideas. Valdés suggested the themes for Ochino's sermons preached in Naples during Lent, 1536. Years later, during his own trial for heresy, Pietro Carnesecchi indicated Ochino as Valdés' closest follower. [22]

Before 1542, when the Holy Office was established to repress heresy, the ideas expressed in the works of Erasmus, Valdés, Luther, Calvin, and other Reformers, were eagerly studied and discussed in Italy. The need to reform the Church had been acutely felt for a long time. In 1524 a group known as the Oratory of Divine Love was created in Rome. Their intent was to reform the Church from within by prayer, meditation, and charity. It was led by Gianpietro Carafa and Count Gaetano da Thiene who were also the founders of the Theatine Order which was devoted to training exemplary priests. The reform of the Roman Church from within and the search for a reunion with the Protestant theologians were goals eagerly sought by Cardinal Gasparo Contarini. In 1536, together with a group that included Carafa, Cortese, Fregoso, Giberti, Pole, and Sadoleto, Contarini contributed to the preparation of a document for Paul III entitled *Consilium delectorum cardinalium et aliarum prelatorum de emendanda ecclesia*. In this document twenty-six abuses were identified for correction.[23] Cardinal Contarini's attempt to compromise with Protestantism, which would have avoided a schism, culminated in the meetings held at Ratisbon in 1541.

The possibility of a compromise was not a dream. Humanistic thought had to some degree eroded the emphasis on the unity between revelation and reason which existed in Scholastic thought.[24] A more direct, intuitive approach gradually emerged. It was linked to Ockhamism and to its opposition to the claims of intellect and reason when not verified by experience.[25] Nominalism brought about a renewal of the Christian charity characteristic of the primitive Church, transcending Scholastic and monastic controversies.[26] Its influence was reflected in the *Devotio Moderna*, whose followers pursued the imitation of Christ while avoiding monastic discipline and the complexities of Scholasticism.[27]

In the early sixteenth century the increase in literacy associated with the invention of the printing press accelerated the diffusion of ideas and enabled more members of society to express their religious thought.[28] Works written by Protestants obtained almost immediate diffusion in Italy. After the 1517 crisis caused by Luther's Theses, there were many Italians who, while wishing to preserve the unity of the Church, were also willing to accept some of the ideas deriving from Protestantism. In his *Guidelines for Concessions to the Lutherans*, Cardinal Cajetan, for instance, went as far as to state that all laws and practices not of divine, but of ecclesiastical origin, should be formally declared as not binding.[29]

And yet the Ratisbon initiative failed. Despite all efforts there were profound differences dividing the two groups. While Contarini and his followers adhered to the doctrine of justification by faith, they also isolated it so that it failed to develop into what the Protestants considered its logical outcome: the radical reform of the Church and the Sacraments.[30] Contarini could not bridge the gap between this position and that of the Protestant group.[31] Thus, in a way so typical of the Italian religious climate of the time, justification by faith remained restricted to the realm of private piety, to the spiritual life of the individual. That was why, in the environment of Italian Evangelism, belief in justification by faith could co-exist with conformity to the existing forms of religious worship. There was widespread hope that a general council would eventually settle the controversial issues and reform the Church.

Introduction

When studying Ochino's religious thought, one should not overlook a third element of importance, that is, the works of the thirteenth- and fourteenth-century Franciscan *Spirituali*. These mystics had emphasized christocentrism, the contemplation of the Cross, and the helplessness of the human soul in its efforts to achieve salvation except through Christ's mediation and through justification by faith. Across the intervening centuries, such themes coincided with some of the teachings of Valdés, Luther, and others.[32]

Ochino's spiritual development during the crucial decade between 1532 and 1542 is undocumented, except for the letters that he wrote later, after his escape, in order to justify or to defend himself. On April 7, 1543, Ochino wrote a reply from Geneva to Girolamo Muzio. The latter had attacked him for an apologetic letter circulating in Ochino's name after his escape. In his reply Ochino remembers how he prayed when he joined the Capuchins: "Lord, if I cannot be saved now, I do not know what else to do." He goes on to say that a few days after becoming a Capuchin he became aware of three fundamental truths: Christ has offered retribution for his elect and he is our only justification; religious vows are not only vain, but downright impious; the Roman Church is an abomination in the eyes of God. Ochino then describes his own subsequent behaviour as external conformity coupled with the cautious dissemination of his new ideas:

> "And though I found some obstacles, yet was I shown a way to survive, by which I could, for the time being, honour God by using the disguise of my habit and my external apparent sanctity of life, and by preaching about grace, Scripture, Christ and his great benefit. I say this in consideration of the extent to which Italy was pervaded by superstition and of the situation in which I found myself. Thus I began to show that we are saved by Christ. The truth is that I perceived Italy's eyes to be so weak that, had I openly shown Christ's great light right away, they would not have been able to endure it. I would have offended Italy to such an extent that the scribes and Pharisees reigning there would have killed me. Thus I thought it was better not to disclose the great light of the Gospel to her immediately, but rather to do it gradually so as to avoid hurting her weak sight. So, adapting my words to her dim eyes, I

preached that we are saved by God's grace through Christ, that he offered retribution for our sins, and that he obtained heaven for us. True, I did not explicitly reveal the impiousness of the kingdom of Antichrist. I did not say: 'There are no other merits, atonements or indulgences except those of Christ, nor is there any Purgatory.' I allowed such conclusions to be reached by those who, by God's grace, had a living awareness of Christ's great benefit. I would never have said: 'You are subjects in the impious kingdom of Antichrist who resides in Rome; the practices of his Church, which is also yours, are extremely corrupt and so too are your doctrines and human religious beliefs. They are wicked; there is no other true religion except that of Christ; you are openly idolatrous and in resorting to the saints as your advocates you offend God, Christ, his Mother and all Heaven.' I could not explain such truths; I just kept silent while waiting for Christ to show me what he wanted to do with me. True, in private I explained the truth to many. Some of them approached me in order to test me, while others did it to satisfy their own interest. A few of them revealed my true faith to the Pope and to the cardinals, feigning opposition to the very things that they had feigned to accept as true when speaking with me in private."[33]

The same attitude appears in his letter to Vittoria Colonna, written from Florence on August 22, 1542, shortly before his escape. In it he weighs the alternatives before him: he can incur suspicion or adapt to preaching Christ disguised by false words.[34] In another letter to the Benedictine Marco da Brescia, Ochino describes his own preaching during those years as an attempt to secretly destroy the labyrinth of Antichrist.[35]

Ochino's fears that he might become the object of suspicion were well founded. As early as 1536 charges of heresy had been laid against him in Naples by other Lenten preachers envious of his fame. Don Pedro di Toledo, the Spanish viceroy, who had been commanded by Charles V to extirpate heresy, had ordered an inquiry and prohibited Ochino from preaching for a short time.[36] Further charges were made against Ochino in 1539 when he again preached in Naples. This time he was accused by the Theatines of twisting the meaning of a quotation from St. Augustine.

Introduction

The quotation should have sounded: "God, who created thee without thy co-operation, will not save thee without thy co-operation." By turning it into an interrogative, Ochino made it sound like a negation of the efficacy of works: "Will not God, who created thee without thy co-operation, save thee also without thy co-operation?"[37] It was observed in a letter dated 1542 that already for two years "Ochino had Christ upon his lips, but no longer mentioned S. Geminiano,"[38] that is, he made no mention of the intercession of saints.

Meanwhile, to his public, Ochino had become the greatest Italian preacher of the period. Cities vied for the privilege of hearing him, especially during Lent, and Paul III himself handled Ochino's preaching commitments. In May, 1540, Ferrante Gonzaga, at that time viceroy of Sicily, tried to secure Ochino as a preacher through the intervention of Vittoria Colonna, who applied to Cardinal Federico Fregoso for help.[39] In 1541 Ochino was reappointed Vicar General of the Capuchins.

During Lent of 1542, in a series of sermons he preached in Venice, Ochino openly defended his old Augustinian friend Giulio della Rovere, who was imprisoned in that city on charges of heresy. These sermons created a crisis that determined the subsequent course of Ochino's life. The Papal Nuncio to Venice, Fabio Mignanelli, temporarily suspended Ochino from preaching.[40] Two months later, when Ochino was in Verona lecturing on St. Paul's Epistles to members of his Order, he received an ominous letter from Cardinal Alessandro Farnese. Paul III requested his presence in Rome, ostensibly to discuss heresy among the Capuchins. Gian Matteo Giberti, with whom Ochino was now on friendly terms, advised him to obey.

In mid-August Ochino began his journey to Rome. On his way through Bologna he stopped to talk with Cardinal Contarini who was dying.[41] In Florence he met his old friend Pietro Martire Vermigli, who was preparing his own escape and who advised him to leave the country. Disregarding the contempt that would fall upon him once his real religious beliefs were made public, Ochino left Italy. He felt, as he stated in his letter to Muzio, that he could no longer be silent and that it was glorious for a Christian to follow Christ, even if that meant being despised by the world.[42]

By September, 1542, he reached Geneva where he was well received by Calvin. His flight had profound repercussions in Italy where reactions ranged from indignation to regret. Vittoria Colonna, Ochino's friend and the self-appointed patroness of the Capuchins after Caterina Cybo's excommunication, commented that "the more he tries to excuse himself, the more he entangles himself. He has forsaken the safe ark of salvation."[43]

Upon reaching Geneva, Ochino felt a sense of relief mixed with admiration for the moral austerity and order in that city.[44] Since he could no longer personally address his Italian audience, he devoted himself to writing sermons and penning replies to critics. Now he could freely express his religious thoughts, which appeared to coincide with those of Calvin. The latter praised Ochino's sound knowledge of theology in a letter to Pellicanus written on April 19, 1543.[45]

Ochino appears to have held no official position in Geneva and in the middle of 1545 he left. After short stays in Basel, where he met Celio Secondo Curione and Sebastiano Castellio, and in Strasbourg, where he met Vermigli again, Ochino reached Augsburg in the autumn. By then he had married a woman from Lucca. He was appointed preacher to the Italian community there and the congregation also included some Germans who could understand Italian because of their frequent business contacts with Venice.[46] Augsburg was prevailingly Protestant though there was still a small Catholic presence. Even so, the local attitude toward the Protestant League was influenced by the fact that the Welser and Fugger banking families did not wish to antagonize Charles V by openly supporting it.

In 1546 the Schmalkaldic War began. By January, 1547, the Imperial army had marched on Augsburg and besieged it. Ochino was charged with fomenting revolt against the Emperor and his surrender was one of the conditions for Augsburg to obtain the Emperor's pardon. Still, Ochino was helped by the city council and he succeeded in making his escape to Constance. From there he went to Zurich and then to Basel, where he stayed with Oporinus, the famous printer, and registered at the University for a brief period. He decided to go once more to Strasbourg and there met Vermigli and Bucer, who were both on the point of leaving for England at the invitation of Archbishop Cranmer. The invitation was also extended to Ochino who reached London with his family in 1547.

During his years in Switzerland and Germany Ochino was a prolific writer. His works include several volumes of Italian sermons, the replies to Girolamo da Lucca, Marco da Brescia, Girolamo Muzio, Ambrogio Catarino, a letter to the Balìa of Siena,[47] the *Image of Antichrist*, an *Exposition of St. Paul's Epistle to the Romans*, another *Exposition of St. Paul's Epistle to the Galatians* and some minor theological works.[48] Some of these works were translated into Latin, German, and French.

Ochino spent some of the most serene years of his life in England. Edward VI was influenced by Archbishop Cranmer's desire to gather representatives from all the Protestant churches in order to form a Council in London that would be the Protestant equivalent of the Council of Trent.[49] Many exiles were invited to London and Bucer was entrusted with the preparation of a plan for the reform of the Church of England.

This ecumenical atmosphere suited Ochino's temperament. In 1549 Dryander wrote to Bullinger: "As far as I can tell, Bernardino has never lived more happily, and worked more successfully than just now. He spends all his leisure hours in literary labours, and he himself says that he works with greater energy and success than ever before."[50] Ochino was appointed prebendary of Canterbury without any obligation to reside there, and was universally admired by the English aristocracy. Anna Cooke, whose father, Anthony Cooke, was Edward VI's tutor, translated fourteen of his sermons on predestination. Princess Elizabeth discussed predestination with Ochino and improved her knowledge of Italian by trying her hand at translating his sermons.[51] Ochino's most important work in this period is the *Tragedy or Dialogue of the Unjust Usurped Primacy of the Bishop of Rome*, written in Latin in 1549 and translated into English by John

Ponet, later Bishop of Winchester. This work was an imitation of Thomas Kirchmayer, who in his *Pammachius* depicts the Pope receiving power from Julian the Apostate. In his work, Ochino confutes the primacy and infallibility of the Pope through a series of dialogues between imaginary characters. The work ends with the victory of Edward VI.

Ochino's happy life in England came to an abrupt end when Edward died in July 1553. With the return of Catholicism, it became necessary for Ochino to flee in order to ensure his own survival. He made his way to Strasbourg, Basel, and finally Geneva where he arrived on October 27, 1553.

The day of Ochino's arrival was the day that Michael Servetus, the Spanish Antitrinitarian, was burnt at the stake there. He openly expressed his disapproval and awakened Calvin's resentment.[52] Ochino only stayed for a short time; however, before leaving he published his *Apologi*. Originally this was a collection of one hundred and ten anti-Catholic short anecdotes, which was enlarged in subsequent editions to number almost five hundred. It was translated into Latin, German, and later also Dutch.

From Geneva Ochino went to Chiavenna and then to Basel where he probably met Castellio and Curione again. In 1555, Martino Muralto and Lelio Sozzini were sent to Basel by the Zurich authorities to offer Ochino the post of pastor of the community which had just emigrated from Locarno to Zurich. Protestantism had existed in Locarno since the early decades of the century. In the 1540's tension arose between the Milanese Inquisition and the Canton of Lugano. Eventually, in January, 1555, the Locarnese Protestants had to emigrate; they reached Zurich on May 12. Ochino accepted the offer and preached to the community for the first time on June 26.

By now Ochino was a highly esteemed Protestant theologian. The fourth volume of his *Prediche* appeared in Basel, probably in 1555. In January, 1556, a Latin pamphlet against Purgatory by Ochino was published in Zurich. It was translated into German by Zwingli's son who, as a consequence, had to justify himself before the Zurich authorities, who feared that the pamphlet might irritate the Catholic Cantons.[53] Ochino's next work, published in January, 1556, was an answer to Joachim Westphal, a Lutheran theologian who had reaffirmed the real presence of the Body of Christ in the Eucharist. In his reply, Ochino sided with the Sacramentarians (Zwingli, Calvin, Bucer, Bullinger, Vermigli and others) who denied the real presence.

Some of Ochino's statements in this work angered the Lutherans. For instance, he claimed that Luther's spiritual development had been gradual[54] and he denied Westphal's claim that the tenets of the Lutheran Church were the only valid ones. He also declared himself disgusted by the hair-splitting controversies of some theologians. The same relativistic, anti-intellectual attitude reappears in his next work, the *Disputa intorno alla presenza del Corpo di Giesu Christo nel Sacramento della Cena*, dedicated to Isabella Bresegna, a refugee from Naples who had belonged to Valdés' circle. The work, published in Basel in 1561 in both Italian and Latin versions, consists of two parts. In the first part Ochino deals with the Eucharist. He shows the tendency, also exhibited by Jacobus Acontius and others, to minimize the essential requisites for salvation in order to avoid endless theological disputes.[55] In the second part, entitled *Tragedia della Messa*, which was probably written some years earlier, Ochino examines the problem of whether a true believer should conform to the practices of the Catholic Church to avoid persecution. He concludes that no rule can be prescribed; in this matter, as in many others, a believer must follow God's inspiration.[56]

An even more critical theological question, that of free will, was the subject of Ochino's next work. The *Labirinti*, dedicated to Elizabeth of England, was published in Italian and in Castellio's Latin translation in Basel in 1561. In it Ochino examined four problems confronting those who believe that human will is free and four problems confronting those who assert predestination. Ochino's wish to avoid dogmatism is apparent in that he offered no clear-cut solution.[57] Instead, he separated the realms of practical reason and religious consciousness, ascribing belief in predestination to the latter.[58] Like Erasmus in his controversy with Luther on the same subject some years earlier, Ochino was bound to displease all parties with his unwillingness to produce an incontrovertible affirmation. His antidogmatism could easily be mistaken for indifference to an important theological issue.

The *Labirinti* was followed by the *Catechism*, published in Basel in 1561, and the fifth and last volume of *Prediche*, in which he criticized the divisions among the Protestants. The Zurich board of pastors, formed by Bullinger, Wolf, and Gwalther, were increasingly alarmed by some of the assertions contained in Ochino's works and in February 1563 they suggested to him to abstain from any further publications unless he had obtained the approval of the board. They failed to inform him that this prohibition extended to cities outside of Zurich.

Ochino's intellectual independence was making his position in Zurich increasingly precarious. The final crisis was precipitated by the publication of his *Dialogi XXX* in Basel in 1563. In June of the same year Beza wrote to Bullinger telling him that the *Dialogi XXX* were full of theological errors.[59] In autumn a formal protest against Ochino's work was lodged by a group of Zurich citizens who had heard it criticized while they were at the Basel fair. In this work Ochino veiledly condemned Servetus' execution as well as the elimination of the Anabaptists. In a dialogue on matrimony, (copied from Lening's *Dialogus Neobuli*, a work commissioned by Philip of Hesse to defend his own polygamy) he failed to condemn polygamy with the required vigour. Instead, he asserted that the final decision lies in the conscience of the individual, thus leaving the entire question in suspense.[60] Altogether he failed to declare himself unequivocally on the side of Protestant orthodoxy.[61] The whole incident now reached the proportions of a scandal. The Zurich pastors could no longer ignore Ochino's statements. He was condemned without being heard and banished from Zurich on November 22, 1563. An old man of seventy-four, he had to depart with his four sons on December 2. He had even been denied permission to remain in Zurich till the end of winter.

Basel and Mulhouse refused to receive him. Ochino then travelled to Nuremberg, where he was allowed to spend the winter. While there he wrote a *Dialogue between Ochino and Carnal Wisdom* in which he defended himself against the charges laid in Zurich. In it he claims for himself the right to search freely for truth.[62] He also accuses Bullinger of being overbearing and ambitious. A reply from the Zurich ministers was not long in appearing; in March, 1564, the *Spongia adversus aspergines Bernardini Ochini* was published to confute Ochino's critiques. At the end of the winter Ochino travelled to Frankfurt am Main.

Examining the situation, a move to Poland appeared quite reasonable. In preceeding years Ochino's works had been quite popular there. Also, the Polish King, Sigismund Augustus, was caught in a complex matrimonial situation; he was seeking a solution by examining different religious opinions with an open-minded attitude.[63] After his arrival in Poland, Ochino enjoyed a short period of considerable success among the tolerant Polish aristocracy.

Many Italian Anabaptists had emigrated to Poland in the hope of finding toleration. This radical group drew some of their inspiration from the medieval *Fraticelli*.[64] Unsurprisingly, Ochino found himself in agreement with some of their beliefs. However, considerable alarm was soon created by the progress of certain extremists, one of whom, Laski, talked of a national Polish church. Cardinal Carlo Borromeo wrote to Cardinal Commendone, the Papal legate in Poland, instructing him to persuade Sigismund Augustus to expel Ochino. A royal edict in the middle of 1564 ordered the expulsion of all non-Catholic foreigners. Ochino had to move once more.

Ochino was struck by the plague at Pinczow and three of his sons died there. On Advent Sunday he left for Moravia where he was sheltered by Niccolò Paruta, an Italian Anabaptist. At the end of 1564 he died in solitude at Schlackau in Moravia. Antonio Baratto, an Italian heretic who had given himself up to the Venetian Inquisition, reported that Paruta told him Ochino had intended to go to

Transylvania. King John Zapolya had been granted power there by the Turks and Ochino had hoped to find there the religious toleration to which he had so vainly aspired for such a long time.[65]

THE *DIALOGI SETTE*

On April 20, 1539 Ochino wrote from Venice to Francesco II Gonzaga in Mantua saying that the *Dialogi* were being copied and would be sent to Luigi Gonzaga, Francesco's ambassador in Venice, as soon as they were finished.[66] As was usual in the sixteenth century, manuscript copies of the *Dialogi*, either individually or together, would have circulated for some time before the work was printed. In his *Rimedio a la pestilente dottrina de Frate Bernardino Ochino. Epistola responsiva diretta al Magnifico Magistrato di Siena*, published in Rome in 1544, Ambrogio Catarino Politi mentions a *Protesto*, which Karl Benrath identified as the seventh dialogue, possibly published in Naples in 1539.[67] Some years ago Benedetto Nicolini discovered a printed version of the third dialogue entitled *Dialogo in che modo la persona debbia reggere bene se stessa*, bearing no place or printer's name and no date. Nicolini conjectured that it might even have been written before 1534, the year in which Ochino joined the Capuchins, and perhaps was revised after Ochino's first meeting with Valdés in 1536. According to Nicolini, the dialogue was probably printed in Naples in 1536 by Johannes Sulzbach.[68]

The first verifiably dated printed edition of one of the *Dialogi* appeared in Asti in 1540. The printer was Francesco Garrone of Leghorn, citizen of Asti. The dialogue is the seventh one, in a version predating the one included in the subsequent editions of the *Dialogi*. It bears the date 1536 at the end and the characters are not Ochino and the Duchess of Camerino, as in subsequent versions, but Ochino and a "gentleman" who remains unidentified.[69] Also in 1540, a collection including the fourth, fifth, sixth and seventh dialogues was printed in Venice by Zoppino. In this edition the date at the end of the seventh dialogue has been changed to 1539. The interlocutors are now Ochino and the Duchess.[70] The popularity of the dialogues is attested to by the fact that in 1540 Zoppino also published the full collection of the *Dialogi*, a copy of which is extant in the Guicciardini Collection at the National Library of Florence. The next two extant complete editions of the *Dialogi* appeared in 1542. One was published by Zoppino in Venice; a copy is preserved in the Guicciardini Collection. The other one was also published in Venice by Bindoni and Pasini; a copy of this edition is preserved in St. John's Library, Cambridge. The above are, so far, the only known copies, after vigorous suppression by the Inquisition.

While the composition of the *Dialogi* may already have begun before 1534, they must have been in their current form by 1540. Works in dialogue form were already a favourite literary form among the fourteenth- and particularly the fifteenth-century humanists.[71] Because of its undogmatic and sometimes elusive quality, the dialogue became a frequent medium for the expression of contrasting religious opinions among the Italian *Spirituali* of the sixteenth century. Erasmus' colloquies no doubt played an important part in popularizing the dialogue as a mode of discussion of religious ideas. Also, one of the most important works relating to Italian Evangelism, Juan de Valdés' *Alfabeto Cristiano*, was written in dialogue form.

By expressing his ideas in the form of an exchange between two characters, Ochino was able to avoid sounding too assertive. In each of the seven dialogues Ochino plays a major role. Ochino invariably depicts himself, or the character representing him, as successfully convincing another character. This may be the Duchess of Camerino, a pupil, or even a soul as in the fifth and sixth dialogues. As happens in Plato's dialogues, Ochino the character meets all possible objections and successfully conveys his message. The affirmative spirit that animates these dialogues enables the reader to appreciate the extent to which Ochino was optimistic about man's potential for self-reform. While there is much in the dialogues that is mystical and ascetic, Ochino does tend to reject the idea of total isolation from the world.

On the contrary, there is a constant need in him to interact and to attract followers.

The fact that justification by works fails to appear in the *Dialogi* has often been noted.[72] Its conspicuous absence enables us to measure the importance Ochino ascribed to justification by faith even before his escape from Italy. Justification by faith, christocentrism, and the Pauline renewal of the inner man constitute three major, constant themes in Ochino's religious thought.[73] Justification by faith is the basis of Christian belief. It is God's gift, the source of the only works which really count for the true believer.[74] Christocentrism permeates Ochino's thought, infusing it with a measure of mysticism. Awareness of Christ's benefit to man and identification with the sufferings of Christ on the Cross are what lead men to salvation. The spiritual marriage of the human soul with Christ results in a mystical ascent to God.[75] Guided by his own inner illumination, the believer becomes spiritually renewed through God's inspiration. With Christ's mediation the need for a structured Church practically disappears, giving way to the real Church, that is, that of the spirit. Ochino's thought is more optimistic about the regeneration of man after the Fall than the thought of Luther or Calvin. Man preserves most of his dignity. Human depravity is not particularly emphasized.[76] Ochino never adopted the belief in predestination that marked the thought of so many other religious thinkers of the time.[77] Thus, justification by faith practically becomes a corollary of human dignity in Ochino's thought.[78]

As may be inferred from this somewhat rapid examination, Ochino is not a systematic thinker.[79] Throughout his life he felt the pressing need to question existing religious beliefs freely while at the same time tending to devalue the role played by rationality in religious faith.[80] His style always remained that of a popular preacher. Imagery and dramatic utterance tend to be more important in his works than the systematic exposition of ideas.[81] Because of the non-dogmatic quality of his religious thought and because of the important role played by justification by faith in his religious outlook, Ochino belongs to the environment of Italian Evangelism, in which he was a leading character for so many years before his flight.[82] In this fluctuating, somewhat enigmatic milieu, the influence of the Protestant Reformers was a major element.[83] At the same time, however, one should not overlook the importance of some significant indigenous currents.[84] For instance, as already noted, Ochino was influenced by Ubertino da Casale and the other Franciscan *Spirituali*.[85] In the *Dialogi* one also finds passages inspired by St. Bonaventure, St. Thomas Aquinas, Duns Scotus, and several others.[86] Because of his intellectual restlessness and inner contradictions, Ochino remains an enigmatic figure, symbolic of the tormented search that underlies Renaissance balance and serenity.

Before a final brief description of the *Dialogi* on an individual basis, it is interesting to look briefly at the life of Caterina Cybo-Varano,[87] Duchess of Camerino, who is present as a character in four of the seven dialogues. Born in 1501, she was the daughter of Franceschetto Cybo, whose father became Pope Innocent VIII, and Maddalena de' Medici, Lorenzo the Magnificent's daughter. At the age of twelve she was betrothed to Giovanni Maria Varano, Duke of Camerino, who was twenty years her senior and the wedding took place before 1520.

Giovanni Maria, a favourite vassal of Leo X who was Caterina's uncle, was a usurper; in 1522 he probably ordered the assassination of his own nephew, Sigismondo, who was legitimately entitled to the duchy. He was denounced by Sigismondo's mother and only narrowly avoided being tried by Adrian VI because of the Pope's death in 1523. Caterina's only child, Giulia, was born in that year.

It was around that time that the Duchess first met Friar Matteo da Bascio, the initiator of the movement that resulted in the creation of the Capuchin Order. Caterina was deeply impressed by the unselfish dedication of Friar Matteo and his followers when Camerino was hit by the plague and she became the self-appointed protectress of the movement. In 1528 she succeeded in obtaining the Bull *Religionis zelus* from her second cousin, Clement VII, that enabled the newly-recognized Capuchins to have their own convents.

Introduction

When Giovanni Maria died of the plague in 1527, Caterina became regent of Camerino. She had to contend with Rodolfo, Giovanni Maria's natural son, who aspired to become duke and who was helped in his attempts by his own brother-in-law, Sciarra Colonna. The Ferrara branch of the Varano family were also Caterina's enemies. The Duchess promised Giulia in marriage to Guidobaldo of Urbino in exchange for military help, but there were many powerful factions opposed to Caterina's plans. Charles V wanted Giulia to marry the son of his own viceroy in Naples. Paul III, even before his election in 1534, proposed his own grandson, Ottaviano Farnese. Eventually Giulia married Guidobaldo. This resulted in the increasing interference of the Duke of Urbino in the affairs of Camerino. In 1535, with Paul III's continuing opposition to the marriage, the situation became critical: Caterina, Giulia, and Guidobaldo were excommunicated. The Duchess left Camerino and spent the rest of her life primarily in Rome and Tuscany. She died in 1557.

Caterina was a cultured woman who was able to read Latin, Greek, and Hebrew. Early in her life she developed a profound interest in religious questions. She may have met Ochino as early as April 1534, when she interceded with Clement to revoke the expulsion of the Capuchins from Rome. In 1536 or 1537 they met again in Florence and continued to be on friendly terms and to meet sporadically until Ochino's flight in 1542. Caterina's interest in religion led her to become acquainted with many *Spirituali*, including Marcantonio Flaminio, Pietro Carnesecchi, and Reginald Pole. For her involvements and acquaintances she was charged with heresy *post mortem*. An entry in the compendium of trials before the Holy Office under Paul III, Julius III, and Paul IV describes her as *"Ducissa Camerini haeretica, sectatrix haereticorum."*

The protagonists of the first and second dialogues are Ochino and Caterina Cybo. In the first dialogue Ochino examines various ways of achieving union with God through love. With imagery revealing the influence of St. Bonaventure, Ochino emphasizes the importance of creation as a mirror of God's attributes. He stresses the need to meditate upon Christ's Passion. On the whole Ochino tends to reject philosophic speculation as a means to approach God. Yet, toward the end of the dialogue, he eventually admits that the intellect plays a considerable part in the process of growing to love God. The work ends with a passage borrowed from Pietro Bembo's speech on love at the end of Book IV of Baldassarre Castiglione's *Book of the Courtier*.

Images deriving from St. Bonaventure are also noticeable in the second dialogue, which deals with the search for inner peace and happiness. For Ochino they cannot depend on material reality. Rather, they arise from the gradual relinquishing of the external world, which results in an ever greater spiritual enrichment. The opinions of some ancient philosophers are quoted as further support for the need to disregard wealth and the comforts of this world.

As already pointed out, the third dialogue may be one of Ochino's earliest published works. The characters are a master and a pupil. The content bears traces of St. Thomas Aquinas in that Ochino ascribes considerable importance to rationality in the search for God. It is man's judgement that guides man's will. Yet, in a structural sense, the dialogue reveals the influence of Juan de Valdés' *Alfabeto Cristiano*. The soul's ascent toward God is in fact presented as a series of steps leading to spiritual perfection. On the whole this dialogue inclines to be more cerebral than mystical.

In the fourth dialogue a man and a woman, who is identified as the Duchess only near the end, discuss the figure of the good thief who died on the Cross with Christ. Ochino's christocentrism, which closely relates to his Franciscan background, is very prominent in this work. The related themes of justification by faith and contemplation of Christ on the Cross are used by Ochino to present the good thief as a symbol of the elect. Numerous passages in this dialogue derive from Ubertino da Casale's *Arbor Vitae Crucifixae Jesu*. Their use by Ochino enhances the ascetic tone of a work that may rightly be described as one of the jewels of Italian Evangelism.

The need to give up all worldly comforts in order to achieve salvation is also the theme of the fifth dialogue. The major character is Christ who persuades a reluctant soul to follow Him. The vivid style of this work, which is full of popular images and metaphors, derives from Ochino's preaching style. The world appears as a tacit third character; a spiteful, evil, malevolent creature bent on destroying man.

In the sixth dialogue a guardian angel instructs a pilgrim soul on how to detach itself from the material world. The precarious state of the human soul during this mortal life is emphasized. The hazards faced in man's progress toward death are vividly described in terms of a dangerous pilgrimage.

Finally we come to the seventh dialogue which was originally dated 1536. It is possible that it was written during the year of Ochino's first meeting with Juan de Valdés. An initial brief dialogue between Ochino and the Duchess is followed by a solemn declaration or spiritual testament. Perhaps the most interesting feature is that Ochino omits any mention of the Church as a guide to spiritual perfection. Instead, the search for inner perfection leading to union with God is a purely personal one. Thus Ochino tends to diminish the importance of the official Church as a collective guide and teacher, instead stressing the importance of the invisible Church of the elect. This emphasis on the need to follow God's inner promptings is remindful of Juan de Valdés.[88]

R. B.

EDITORIAL NOTE

For this translation the following editions have been consulted:

Dialogi quattro Venice: Zoppino, 1540;
Dialogo della Divina Professione, that is, the seventh dialogue, Asti: Garrone, 1540;[89]

Dialogi sette, Venice: Zoppino, 1542;

Dialoghi Sette del Rev. Padre Frate Bernardino Ochino Senese, Generale dei Frati Cappuccini. Edited by E. Comba(?). Biblioteca della Riforma Italiana, vol. 5. Florence: Tipografia Claudiana, 1884;[90]

"Dialogue Concerning the Thief on the Cross." In *Reform Thought in Sixteenth-century Italy.* Edited and translated by E. G. Gleason. Ann Arbor: Scholars Press, 1981. This is the only existing translation into English of one of Ochino's *Dialogi;*

I "Dialogi Sette" e altri scritti del tempo della fuga. Edited by U. Rozzo. Turin: Claudiana, 1985. This is the only reliable modern edition of the *Dialogi* and it became available when most of this translation had already been completed.

The most significant minor variants occurring in the Garrone edition of the seventh dialogue are pointed out in the notes. The overall aim has been to strive for the greatest possible clarity while still being faithful to the original text. The style of the original text has been followed with respect to capitalization.

Scriptural quotations and allusions have been translated in the way in which Ochino quotes them. That is often quite different from the standard text of the Vulgate because he may have been quoting from memory.

R. B.

NOTES TO INTRODUCTION

1. F. Cuthbert, O.S.F.C., *The Capuchins. A Contribution to the History of the Counter-reformation* (Port Washington, N.Y.: Kennikat Press, 1971), vol. 1, 130-31.

2. R. H. Bainton, *Bernardino Ochino esule e riformatore senese del Cinquecento*, trans. E. Gianturco (Florence: G. C. Sansoni, 1940), 6, 48-49.

3. B. Feliciangeli, *Notizie e documenti sulla vita di Caterina Cybo-Varano duchessa di Camerino* (Camerino: Tipografia Savini, 1891), 251; B. Nicolini, *Il pensiero di Bernardino Ochino* (Naples: R. Riciardi, 1939), 96-97.

4. B. Nicolini, "Bernardino Ochino. Saggio biografico," *Biblion. Rivista di filologia, storia e bibliografia*, 1 (1959): 6.

5. Nicolini, "Bernardino Ochino," 9; F. Callaey, "Bernardino Ochino fautore della pseudo-Riforma," *L'Italia Francescana*, 6 (1931): 4-5.

6. Nicolini, "Bernardino Ochino," 17: "Mi saria stato grato, quanto al respeto mio proprio, fussero venuti più presto, benchè forse così è stata la volontà di Dio."

7. Bainton, *Bernardino Ochino*, 20-21: "E s'alcuno dicesse, ergo riformisi tutta la detta congregazione, dico che questo ad ogni umana potenza è *simpliciter* impossibile per la grande moltitudine dei pessimi soggetti che ci son dentro, i quali tengono talmente oppressi i buoni che in nulla cosa li lasciano valere . . .''; see E. G. Gleason, "5. Gianpietro Carafa, Memorial to Pope Clement VII (1532)," in *Reform Thought in Sixteenth-century Italy* (Ann Arbor, Mich.: Scholars Press, 1981), 55-80 for an English translation.

8. U. Rozzo, "Nuovi contributi su Bernardino Ochino," *Bollettino della Società di Studi Valdesi*, 146 (1979): 60-62.

9. Cuthbert, *Capuchins*, vol. 1, 25.

10. K. Benrath, *Bernardino Ochino of Siena. A Contribution towards the History of the Reformation*, trans. H. Zimmern (New York: Robert Carter and Bros., 1877), 12.

11. Edouard d'Alençon, O.F.M.Cap., ed., *Primigeniae Legislationis Ordinis Fratrum Minorum Capuccinorum Textus Originales seu Constitutiones Anno 1536 Ordinatae et Anno 1552 Recognitae cum*

Historica Introductione Copiosisque Adnotationibus (Rome: Curia generalis Fr. minorum capuccinorum, 1928), 49 et seq. Ochino was directly involved in the revision of the Constitution in 1536; see P. McNair, *Peter Martyr in Italy. An Anatomy of Apostasy* (Oxford: Oxford University Press, 1967), 34.

12. This was an important office that empowered him to decide points of discipline.

13. The information is quoted in Nicolini, "Bernardino Ochino," 19.

14. Translated for this introduction from Pietro Aretino, *Il secondo libro delle lettere*, ed. F. Nicolini (Bari: Gius. Laterza e figli, 1916), Part 1, 122-23.

15. G. Manzoni, ed., "Estratto del processo di Pietro Carnesecchi," *Miscellanea di storia italiana*, 10 (1870): 516 et seq. Carnesecchi also confessed that he had had two or three private meetings with Ochino; see McNair, *Peter Martyr*, 33.

16. The passage, which derives from Graziani's biography of Cardinal Commendone, is quoted in Benrath, *Ochino of Siena*, 17.

17. McNair, *Peter Martyr*, 17 et seq.

18. D. de Sta. Teresa, *Juan de Valdés 1498(?)-1541* (Rome: Gregorian University, 1957), 65 et seq.; for Erasmus' influence on Valdés see M. Bataillon, *Erasme et l'Espagne; recherches sur l'histoire spirituelle du XVIe siècle* (Paris: E. Droz, 1937), ch. 7, for the differences between Erasmus' and Valdés' religious thought.

19. J. C. Nieto, *Juan de Valdés and the Origins of the Spanish and Italian Reformation* (Geneva: Droz, 1970), 266: "Experience and not obedience or subjection of the intellect to the authority of the Church and dogma is what Valdés propounds."

20. See Manzoni, ed., "Estratto del processo," 533: "Imperò, quando io tenevo così non havevo ancora considerato quelle conclusioni che si potevano dedurre da cotale principio, perchè Valdés insegnava tale dottrina semplicemente et senza pure accennare, non che toccare, alcune delle conclusioni sudette, come quello che o non le teneva esso, o vero le dissimulava, per non dare scandalo alli suoi discipoli . . . ."

21. McNair, *Peter Martyr*, 25 et seq.

22. Manzoni, ed., "Estratto del Processo," 196, 535.

23. McNair, *Peter Martyr*, 15; see Gleason, "6. Proposal of a Select Committee of Cardinals and other Prelates Concerning the

Reform of the Church, Written and Presented by Order of His Holiness Pope Paul III (1537)," in *Reform Thought*, 81-100.

24. C. Trinkaus, "The Religious Thought of the Italian Humanists, and the Reformers: Anticipation or Autonomy?" in C. Trinkaus and H. A. Oberman, eds., *The Pursuit of Holiness in Late Medieval and Renaissance Religion* (Leiden: Brill, 1974), 344.

25. H. A. Oberman, "The Shape of Late Medieval Thought: the Birthpangs of the Modern Era," in Trinkaus and Oberman, eds., *Pursuit of Holiness*, 14; see Bataillon, *Erasme et l'Espagne*, 19, on the influence of nominalism at Alcalá: "Surtout l'enseignement théologique et le sentiment religieux durent être confirmés par le nominalisme dans les tendances fidéistes alors régnantes."

26. H.A. Oberman, *Masters of the Reformation. The Emergence of a New Intellectual Climate in Europe*, trans. D. Martin (Cambridge: Cambridge University Press, 1981), 46.

27. ibid., 7.

28. ibid., 187.

29. J. Wicks, S.J., ed. and trans., *Cajetan Responds. A Reader in Reformation Controversy* (Washington: The Catholic University of America Press, 1978), 202.

30. P. Matheson, *Cardinal Contarini at Regensburg* (Oxford: Clarendon Press, 1972), 178-79; for a brief general account of the Reformation movement in Italy, see Bainton, "The Reformation in Italy," in *Women of the Reformation in Germany and Italy* (Minneapolis: Augsburg Publishing House, 1971), 165-69.

31. D. Fenlon, *Heresy and Obedience in Tridentine Italy. Cardinal Pole and the Counter Reformation* (Cambridge: Cambridge University Press, 1972), 65.

32. R. Belladonna, "Bernardino Ochino's Fourth Dialogue (*Dialogo del Ladrone in Croce*) and Ubertino da Casale's *Arbor Vitae*: Adaptation and Ambiguity," *Bibliothèque d'Humanisme et Renaissance*, 47, no. 1 (1985): 125-45. Ochino was an avid reader of Protestant works. Bernardino da Colpetrazzo, a contemporary fellow-Capuchin, wrote that Ochino's cell was full of prohibited books; see also C. Cargnoni, "Bernardino Ochino," in *Dictionnaire de spiritualité ascétique et mystique*, ed. M. Viller, S.J. (Paris: Gabriel Beauchesne et ses Fils, 1982), vol. 11, col. 580.

33. Translated for this introduction from C. Cantù, "Discorso XXIII. Frà Bernardino Ochino," in *Gli eretici d'Italia. Discorsi storici* (Turin: Unione tipografico-editrice, 1865), vol 2, 49-50; U. Rozzo, ed., "IX. Lettera a Gerolamo Muzio (*Responsio ad Mutium Justinopolitanum*)," in *I "Dialogi Sette" e altri scritti del tempo della fuga* (Turin: Claudiana, 1985), 130-36.

34. Cantù, *Gli eretici d'Italia*, 46: "Da poi, che farei più in Italia? Predicar sospetto, e predicar Cristo mascherato in gergo . . ."; see also Rozzo, ed., "IV. Lettera a Vittoria Colonna," in *I "Dialogi Sette"*, 123-24.

35. B. Nicolini, ed., *Lettere di negozi del pieno Cinquecento* (Bologna: Pàtron, 1965), 64: "Nam paulatim et quasi clanculum ac per cuniculos Antichristi labyrintum destruendo Christi regnum erigebam."

36. Benrath, *Ochino of Siena*, 69.

37. ibid.; D. Bertrand-Barraud, *Les idées philosophiques de Bernardin Ochin de Sienne* (Paris: J. Vrin, 1924), 5.

38. The remark is contained in a letter written to Cardinal Morone on July 3, 1542, quoted in Benrath, *Ochino of Siena*, 70.

39. Vittoria Colonna Marchesa di Pescara, *Carteggio*, ed. Ermanno Ferrero and Giuseppe Müller (Turin: Loescher, 1892²), no. 113, 188-89. The letter is dated May 13, 1540.

40. Benrath, *Ochino of Siena*, 94-95. Ochino had already been summoned once by Cardinal Mignanelli during the same period because he had been reported by spies to have made heretical statements.

41. Bainton, *Bernardino Ochino*, 53-54. There are various versions of Ochino's meeting with Contarini.

42. Cantù, *Gli eretici d'Italia*, 51: "Mi suadeva la prudenza umana a più presto morire che viver così infame, ma lo spirito rispondeva, che è somma gloria del cristiano vivere per Cristo e con Cristo, infame al mondo."

43. Quoted in Benrath, *Ochino of Siena*, 130; see G. Fragnito, "Gli 'Spirituali' e la fuga di Bernardino Ochino," *Rivista Storica Italiana*, 84, no. 3 (1972): 777-881; see Rozzo, ed., *I "Dialogi Sette"*, 18-19 for the attempts to suppress Ochino's works immediately after his escape.

44. Bernardino Ochino, "Predica X," *Prediche di Bernardino Ochino da Siena. Novellamente Ristampate et con grande diligentia rivedute*

et corrette. Con la sua tavola nel fine [Basel, 1562], pages unnumbered: ". . . qui non sono sodomie, sacrilegij, incesti, stupri, adulterij, ne tante spurcitie, si come sono in molti altri luoghi dove sono stato, qui non sono ruffiani, ne meretrici, in fino alla semplice fornicatione sarebbe punita . . . ."

45. Benrath, *Ochino of Siena*, 152.

46. Bainton, *Bernardino Ochino*, 77.

47. For the letter to the Balìa see V. Marchetti, *Gruppi ereticali senesi del Cinquecento* (Florence: La Nuova Italia, 1975), 1-15, 247-57; and Rozzo, ed., "X. Epistola ai Signori di Balìa della Città di Siena," in *I "Dialogi Sette"*, 136-45.

48. See the lists of Ochino's writings in Benrath's, Bainton's, and Rozzo's works.

49. Bainton, *Bernardino Ochino*, 94.

50. Benrath, *Ochino of Siena*, 188.

51. Bainton, *Bernardino Ochino*, 90.

52. ibid., 101.

53. Benrath, *Ochino of Siena*, 229; Bainton, *Bernardino Ochino*, 114.

54. Quoted in Benrath, *Ochino of Siena*, 234: ". . . when Martin already perceived that the Papal indulgences were vain lies and deceits, he did not yet understand that Christ is our only justification."; see also Bainton, *Bernardino Ochino*, 115.

55. See J. Lecler, S.J., *Toleration and the Reformation*, trans. T. L. Westow (New York: Association Press, 1960), 365 et seq.

56. Quoted in Benrath, *Ochino of Siena*, 248-49: "Participation in the mass is no indifferent action for a Christian, since it implies the recognition of the Antichristian kingdom, but if abstaining from it is followed by persecution, then let everyone regard God's voice in himself. If God wishes him to stay, he must do so, but if God's voice tells him that his time is not yet come, then he may fly. Did not Christ fly when His time had not yet come, and did not the apostles and many pious men follow His example?"

57. Bainton, *Bernardino Ochino*, 121-22.

58. Benrath, *Ochino of Siena*, 250-51.

59. ibid., 266.

60. Ochino's tendency to ascribe more importance to divine inspiration than to the literal interpretation of Scripture greatly irritated Bullinger. See Bainton, *Bernardino Ochino*, 140.

61. Benrath ascribes Ochino's tendency to follow the promptings of the Spirit largely to the influence of Sebastiano Castellione and Lelio Sozzini. See *Ochino of Siena*, 259; see also Rozzo, ed., *I "Dialogi Sette"*, 28: "Il tema dell'*inspiratione*, meglio della *divina inspiratione*, che è cogente per il "vero" cristiano, si trova . . . presente in diversi esponenti del rinnovamento religioso in Italia, pur provenienti da dissimili esperienze personali e teologiche . . . ."

62. See the passage quoted in Benrath, *Ochino of Siena*, 280: "The true Churches of Christ . . . cannot complain of me, because I carefully examine such doubts as may present themselves. But if the arguments of some, which I reproduce in the *Dialogues*, prove weak, and the counter arguments strong, I am not to blame for this, for I cannot overcome good arguments. The fault lies with those who desire that errors should be defended in the name of truth."; see Cargnoni, "Bernardino Ochino," col. 579 for a description of Ochino as the Ulysses of Italian reform.

63. Sigismund Augustus, a widower, married Barbara Radziwill, a Calvinist, who died five days after the wedding. He then married his first wife's sister. Unable to obtain heirs, he ascribed this to God's punishment for marrying his own sister-in-law and he tried to obtain a divorce. See Bainton, *Bernardino Ochino*, 133.

64. ibid., 160: "Molta parte dell'anabattismo s'accordava con le credenze da lui professate durante tutta la vita. Il cammino dell'anabattismo era stato spianato dai movimenti religiosi dell'evo medio, e i Moravi consideravano i Fraticelli come i loro antenati spirituali."

65. ibid., 161.

66. B. Nicolini, *Bernardino Ochino e la Riforma in Italia* (Naples: R. Riciardi, 1935), 202.

67. Rozzo, "Nuovi contributi," 54.

68. B. Nicolini, "D'una sconosciuta edizione di un dialogo dell'Ochino," in *Aspetti della vita religiosa politica e letteraria*, vol. 2 of *Studi cinquecenteschi* (Bologna: Tamari, 1974), 27-31.

69. See Rozzo, "Nuovi contributi," 77, for an attempt to identify the character as Bartolomeo Carli Piccolomini.

70. J. Tedeschi and P. McNair, "New Light on Ochino," *Bibliothèque d'Humanisme et Renaissance*, 35, no. 2 (1973): 289-301.

71. D. Marsh, *The Quattrocento Dialogue. Classical Tradition and Humanist Innovation* (Cambridge, Mass.: Harvard University Press, 1980), 5 et seq.

72. Benrath, *Ochino of Siena*, 84; Bertrand-Barraud, *Les idées philosophiques*, 6.

73. Cargnoni, "Bernardino Ochino," cols. 582-87.

74. Cf. Juan de Valdés, *Alfabeto Cristiano. Dialogo con Giulia Gonzaga*, ed. B. Croce (Bari: Gius. Laterza e figli, 1938), 49: "E sappiate, signora, che così come il fuoco non può lasciare di scaldare, così la fede viva non può lasciare d'oprare opre di carità, e v'avete da immaginare che la fede è come un albero e la carità è il frutto dell'albero."; Benedetto da Mantova, *Il Beneficio di Cristo con le versioni del secolo XVI. Documenti e testimonianze*, ed. S. Caponetto (Florence: Sansoni, 1972), 44: "Adunque la fede, che giustifica, è come una fiamma di fuoco, la qual non può se non risplendere; e, come è vero che la fiamma sola abbruscia il legno senza l'aiuto della luce, e nondimeno la fiamma non può esser senza luce, così è vero che la fede sola estingue e abbruscia i peccati senza lo aiuto delle opere."

75. Cf. Valdés, *Alfabeto Cristiano*, 71: "E sappiate certo che non è luogo nessuno dove meglio possiate conoscere Iddio che in Cristo crocifisso"; B. da Mantova, *Beneficio di Cristo*, 27: "Tanto opera questa fede santa e viva, che colui, il quale crede che Cristo abbia tolto sopra di sè li suoi peccati, diventa simile a Cristo, e vince il peccato, la morte, il diavolo e lo inferno. . . . Dio ha sposato il suo dilettissimo Figliuolo con l'anima fidele, la qual non avendo cosa alcuna che fusse sua propria se non il peccato, il Figliuol di Dio non si è disdegnato di pigliarla per diletta sposa con la propria dote, ch'è il peccato . . . ."

76. Cargnoni, "Bernardino Ochino," col. 587.

77. Bertrand-Barraud, *Les idées philosophiques*, 27: ". . . car le calvinisme professait une doctrine rigoureuse de la prédestination qu'Ochin n'a jamais adoptée."; Rozzo, ed., *I "Dialogi Sette"*, 15-16: "Certo gli anni a Ginevra, . . . a diretto contatto con la prorompente personalità di Calvino e nella capitale del rigorismo riformato, saranno comunque fondamentali per la sua storia personale e per le sue scelte future, ma in buona sos-

tanza l'Ochino non riuscirà ad inserirsi pienamente e definitivamente nella rigida organizzazione ginevrina . . . ."

78. D. Cantimori, *Bernardino Ochino uomo del Rinascimento e riformatore* (Pisa: Pacini Mariotti, 1929), 33.

79. Bertrand-Barraud, *Les idées philosophiques*, 110: "Ochin était un homme doué d'une intelligence exceptionellement souple, alerte et fine, mais à laquelle manquait une force de conception suffisante pour ordonner dans le cadre de la spéculation generale des intuitions fulgurantes."

80. ibid., 110: "Il n'a lâché bride à la raison que pour avoir finalement sujet de l'humilier."

81. ibid., 116: ". . . sa pensée si souvent flottante s'extériorise en images plus qu'elle ne se concentre en concepts, et il s'addresse moins à la raison qu'au coeur . . ."; Cargnoni, "Bernardino Ochino," col. 588: ". . . il est au fond resté un predicateur populaire."

82. See Fenlon, *Heresy and Obedience*, 19-20, for the following attempt to describe Italian Evangelism: ". . . drawing upon spiritual currents already existing not only in Italy, but in Europe as a whole, [it] sought to adapt the insights of Luther, and later (in its more radical exponents) of Calvin, to the practice of a Christianity not externally different from that of Rome. Its spiritual axis was the doctrine of justification by faith. Such a movement, by its very nature, eludes more concrete definition. Most of its adherents expected their views to be ratified by a General Council. Some, no doubt, were consciously heretical or . . . became so."

83. See Cargnoni, "Bernardino Ochino," cols. 588-89.

84. See C. Ginzburg, "Folklore, magia, religione," in *I caratteri originali*, vol. 1 of *Storia d'Italia*, ed. R. Romano and C. Vivanti (Turin: G. Einaudi, 1972³), 603 et seq.

85. For the influence of the medieval *Spirituali* on the sixteenth-century Capuchins see F. Callaey, *L'infiltration des idées franciscaines spirituelles chez les frères-mineurs capucins au XVIe siècle* (Rome: Tipografia del Senato, 1924).

86. Cargnoni, "Bernardino Ochino," col. 587.

87. For Caterina Cybo, see Feliciangeli, *Notizie e documenti*; also Bainton, "Caterina Cibo," in *Women of the Reformation*, 187-98.

88. For the importance ascribed by Valdés to divine inspiration see V. Marchetti, "Un'epistola inedita di Juan de Valdés sopra i 'movimenti dello spirito'," *Archivio Storico Italiano*, 129 (1972): 505-18.
89. I am indebted to Prof. Ugo Rozzo for a xerox of the Garrone edition, and to Prof. John Tedeschi for a xerox of the 1542 edition of the *Dialogi Sette* which he supplied including his own notes of the variants appearing in the *Dialogi Quattro*.
90. See Rozzo, ed., *I "Dialogi Sette"*, 21.

SELECT BIBLIOGRAPHY

Ochino's Pre-exilic Works:

DIALOGO IN CHE MODO LA PERSONA DEBBIA REGGERE BENE SE STESSA. Composto per lo Reverendo padre frate Bernardino da Siena de l'ordine de frati minori nominati CAPUCINI devoto et illuminato theologo. No place, printer's name or date. In the Vatican Library, Ferraiol V 7622.

DYALOGO DELLA DIVINA PROFESSIONE di Frate Bernardino da Siena della Congregatione de Capuccini dove sono interlocutori un Predicatore et un Gentilhuomo. Asti: Francesco Garrone, 1540. In the Accademia delle Scienze, Turin.

DIALOGI QUATTRO del Reveren. Frate Bernardino da Siena detto il Scapuzzino, ove si contengono del Ladrone in Croce qual salvossi, del pentirsi presto, del peregrinaggio per andare al Paradiso, della Divina professione con un Spirituale testamento: Opera nuova con somma diligenza corretta, Historiata, e nuovamente stampata. Venice: Nicolò d'Aristotile detto il Zoppino, 1540. In the Newberry Library, Chicago.

DIALOGI SETTE del Reverendo Padre Frate Bernardino Ochino Senese Generale di frati Capuzzini. Venice: Nicolò d'Aristotile detto il Zoppino, 1540. In the Guicciardini Collection 23-3-23, Biblioteca Nazionale Centrale, Florence.

DIALOGI SETTE del Reverendo Padre Frate Bernardino Ochino Senese Generale di frati Capuzzini. Venice: Nicolò d'Aristotile detto il Zoppino, 1542. In the Guicciardini Collection 2) 2-6-21, Biblioteca Nazionale Centrale, Florence.

DIALOGI del Reverendo Padre Frate Bernardino Ochino Senese Generale di frati Capuzzini. Nuovamente stampati, et con somma diligentia corretti. Venice: Francesco di Alessandro Bindoni and Mapheo Pasini, 1542. In St. John's College Library, Cambridge.

Select Bibliography

PREDICHE NOVE predicate dal Reverendo Padre Frate Bernardino Occhino Senese Generale dell'ordine di frati Capuzzini nella Inclita Citta di Vinegia. Venice: Nicolò d'Aristotile detto il Zoppino, 1541. In the Banco Rari 250, Biblioteca Nazionale Centrale, Florence.

PREDICHE del Reverendo Padre Frate Bernardino Occhino Senese Generale dell'ordine di frati Capuzzini, predicate nella Inclita Citta di Vinegia. Venice: Francesco di Alessandro Bindoni and Mapheo Pasini, 1541. In the Guicciardini Collection 2-6-21, Biblioteca Nazionale Centrale, Florence.

PREDICHE, predicate dal R. Padre Frate Bernardino da Siena dell'ordine de Frati Capuccini. Ristampate Novamente. Et giontovi unaltra Predicha. Venice: Bernardino de Viano de Lexona Vercellese, 1541. In the British Museum Library.

Dialoghi Sette del Rev. Padre Frate Bernardino Ochino Senese, Generale dei Frati Cappuccini, edited by E. Comba(?). Biblioteca della Riforma Italiana, vol. 5. Florence: Tipografia Claudiana, 1884.

I "Dialogi Sette" e altri scritti del tempo della fuga, edited by U. Rozzo. Turin: Claudiana, 1985.

Works on Ochino:

Bainton, R. *Bernardino Ochino, esule e riformatore senese del Cinquecento, 1487-1563.* Translated by E. Gianturco. Florence: G. C. Sansoni, 1941.

Belladonna, R. "Bernardino Ochino's Fourth Dialogue (Dialogo del Ladrone in Croce) and Ubertino da Casale's *Arbor Vitae*: Adaptation and Ambiguity." *Bibliothèque d'Humanisme et Renaissance* 47, no. 1 (1985): 125-45.

Benrath, K. *Bernardino Ochino of Siena: a Contribution towards the History of the Reformation.* Translated by H. Zimmern. New York: Robert Carter and Bros., 1877.

Bertrand-Barraud, D. *Les idées philosophiques de Bernardin Ochin de Sienne.* Paris: J. Vrin, 1924.

Callaey, F. "Bernardino Ochino fautore della pseudo-Riforma." *L'Italia Francescana* 6 (1931): 156-83.

Select Bibliography

Cantimori, D. *Bernardino Ochino uomo del Rinascimento e riformatore*. Pisa: Pacini Mariotti, 1929.

Cargnoni, C. "Bernardino Ochino." In *Dictionnaire de spiritualité ascétique et mystique*, vol. 11. Edited by M. Viller, S.J. Paris: Gabriel Beauchesne et ses Fils, 1982, cols. 575-90.

Fragnito, G. "Gli 'Spirituali' e la fuga di Bernardino Ochino." *Rivista Storica Italiana* 84 (1972): 777-813.

McNair, P. "Ochino on Sedition. An Italian Dialogue of the Sixteenth Century." *Italian Studies* 15 (1960): 36-49.

Negri, P. "Note e documenti per la storia della Riforma in Italia, 2. Bernardino Ochino." *Atti della R. Accademia di Scienze di Torino* 47 (1912): 57-81.

Nicolini, B. *Bernardino Ochino e la Riforma in Italia*. Naples: R. Riciardi, 1935.

———. *Il pensiero di Bernardino Ochino*. Naples: R. Riciardi, 1939.

———. "Bernardino Ochino. Saggio biografico." *Biblion. Rivista di filologia, storia e bibliografia* 1 (1959): 5-25, 89-114.

Piccolomini, P. "Due lettere inedite di Bernardino Ochino." *Archivio della R. Società Romana di Storia Patria* 28 (1905): 201-07.

Rozzo, U. "Nuovi contributi su Bernardino Ochino." *Bollettino della Società di Studi Valdesi* 146 (1979): 51-83.

———. "Antonio da Pinerolo e Bernardino Ochino." *Rivista di Storia e Letteratura religiosa* 19 (1982): 341-64.

Solmi, E. "La fuga di Bernardino Ochino secondo i documenti dell'Archivio Gonzaga di Mantova." *Bullettino Senese di Storia Patria* 15 (1908): 3-78.

Tedeschi, J., and P. McNair. "New Light on Ochino." *Bibliothèque d'Humanisme et Renaissance* 35, no. 2 (1973): 289-301.

Works Mentioning Ochino:

Arsenio d'Ascoli. *La predicazione dei Cappuccini nel Cinquecento in Italia*. Loreto (Ancona): Libreria "S. Francesco d'Assisi", 1956. An interesting attempt to evaluate Ochino's preaching in relation to the Capuchin tradition.

Cantù, C. *Gli eretici d'Italia. Discorsi storici.* 3 vols. Turin: Unione tipografico-editrice, 1865-66. A classic reference work for the history of the Reformation in Italy.

F. Cuthbert, O.S.F.C. *The Capuchins. A Contribution to the History of the Counter-reformation.* 2 vols. Port Washington, N.Y.: Kennikat Press, 1971. A classic history of the Order containing some interesting remarks on Ochino.

Gleason, E. G. *Reform Thought in Sixteenth-century Italy.* Ann Arbor, Mich.: Scholars Press, 1981. An excellent introduction to the topic, containing a translation of the fourth dialogue and a good bibliography on Italian Evangelism.

Manzoni, G., ed. "Estratto del processo di Pietro Carnesecchi." *Miscellanea di storia italiana* 10 (1870): 187-551. Fascinating account of the trial for heresy of a key figure of Italian Evangelism.

Marchetti, V. *Gruppi ereticali senesi del Cinquecento.* Florence: La Nuova Italia, 1975. An important work on the diffusion and repression of Protestant ideas in Siena. Contains a chapter on Ochino.

McNair, P. *Peter Martyr Vermigli in Italy. An Anatomy of Apostasy.* Oxford: Oxford University Press, 1967. A fundamental study of Vermigli's life before his flight in 1542.

Nicolini, B. *Illustrazione di un documento e vicende di un carteggio.* Vol. 4 of *Quaderni della Scuola di paleografia ed archivistica.* Bologna: Archivio di Stato, 1963. Contains information on important aspects of Ochino's life.

————. *Studi cinquecenteschi.* 2 vols. Bologna: Tamari, 1968-74. Contains information on important aspects of Ochino's life.

Nicolini, B., ed. *Lettere di negozi del pieno Cinquecento.* Bologna: Pàtron, 1965. Contains information on important aspects of Ochino's life.

Works of Related Interest:

Bainton, R. *Women of the Reformation in Germany and Italy.*

Minneapolis: Augsburg Publishing House, 1971. Important for the life of Caterina Cybo-Varano.

Bataillon, M. *Erasme et l'Espagne; recherches sur l'histoire spirituelle du XVIe siècle*. Paris: E. Droz, 1937. A fundamental work on Erasmus' influence in Spain.

Benedetto da Mantova. *Il Beneficio di Cristo*. Edited by S. Caponetto. Florence: Sansoni, 1972. An essential work for Italian Evangelism. Formerly attributed to Aonio Paleario.

Callaey, F. *L'infiltration des idées franciscaines spirituelles chez les frères-mineurs capucins au XVIe siècle*. Rome: Tipografia del Senato, 1924. The influence of the medieval Franciscan Spirituali on the sixteenth-century Capuchins.

Cantimori, D. *Prospettive di storia ereticale italiana del Cinquecento*. Bari: Laterza, 1960. A compendium of the history of the Italian reform movement.

_____. *Eretici italiani del Cinquecento*. Florence: G. C. Sansoni, 1939; reprinted Florence, 1967. One of the best studies of some leading unorthodox religious thinkers.

_____. *Umanesimo e religione nel Rinascimento*. Turin: G. Einaudi, 1975. A collection of essays abounding in interesting insights into the role of religion in Renaissance Italy.

D. da Sta. Teresa. *Juan de Valdés 1498(?)-1541*. Rome: Gregorian University, 1957. A fundamental biography.

Edouard d'Alençon, O.F.M.Cap., ed. *Primigeniae Legislationis Ordinis Fratrum Minorum Capuccinorum Textus Originales seu Constitutiones Anno 1536 Ordinatae et Anno 1552 Recognitae cum Historica Introductione Copiosisque Adnotationibus*. Rome: Curia generalis Fr. minorum capuccinorum, 1928. Annotated edition of the earliest Constitutions of the Capuchin Order.

Feliciangeli, B. *Notizie e documenti sulla vita di Caterina Cibo-Varano duchessa di Camerino*. Camerino: Tipografia Savini, 1891. The most important source of information on Caterina Cybo-Varano.

Fenlon, D. *Heresy and Obedience in Tridentine Italy. Cardinal Pole and the Counter Reformation*. Cambridge: Cambridge

University Press, 1972. A useful account of the environment of the *Spirituali,* particularly of one of its key figures.

Ginzburg, C. *Il nicodemismo. Simulazione e dissimulazione religiosa nell'Europa del '500.* Turin: G. Einaudi, 1970. An important work on sixteenth-century religious dissimulation.

Ginzburg, C., and A. Prosperi. *Giochi di pazienza. Un seminario sul "Beneficio di Cristo".* Turin: G. Einaudi, 1975. The results of a series of seminars on the *Beneficio di Cristo* conducted by the authors.

Grendler, P. *The Roman Inquisition and the Venetian Press 1540-1605.* Princeton: Princeton University Press, 1977. A valuable account of the circulation of clandestine religious literature in sixteenth-century Italy.

Jung, E.-M. "On the Nature of Evangelism in sixteenth-century Italy." *Journal of the History of Ideas* 14 (1953): 511-27. A stimulating article.

Lecler, J., S.J. *Toleration and the Reformation.* Translated by T. L. Westow. New York: Association Press, 1960. On the emergence of toleration in sixteenth-century religious thought.

Marchetti, V. "Un epistola inedita di Juan de Valdés sopra i 'movimenti dello spirito'." *Archivio Storico Italiano* 129 (1972): 505-18. An enlightening article on a specific aspect of Valdés' thought.

Marsh, D. *The Quattrocento Dialogue. Classical Tradition and Humanist Innovation.* Cambridge, Mass.: Harvard University Press, 1980. The cultural background to the humanistic dialogue.

Matheson, P. *Cardinal Contarini at Regensburg.* Oxford: Clarendon Press, 1972. An account of Cardinal Contarini's position during his attempt at reunion.

McLelland, J. C., ed. *Peter Martyr Vermigli and Italian Reform.* Waterloo, Ont.: Wilfrid Laurier University Press, 1980. An interesting collection of essays relating to Ochino's friend and his times.

Nieto, J. C. *Juan de Valdés and the Origins of the Spanish and Italian Reformation.* Geneva: Droz, 1970. An important attempt to analyze the similarities and differences between Valdés and the Reformers.

Oberman, H. A. *Masters of the Reformation. The Emergence of a New Intellectual Climate in Europe.* Translated by D. Martin. Cambridge: Cambridge University Press, 1981. A study of the way in which the Reformation changed the European intellectual outlook.

Rotondò, A. "Atteggiamenti della vita italiana del Cinquecento. La pratica nicodemitica." *Rivista Storica Italiana* 79 (1967): 991-1030. An important account of religious dissimulation in sixteenth-century Italy.

Trinkaus, C., and H. A. Oberman, eds. *The Pursuit of Holiness in Late Medieval and Renaissance Religion.* Leiden: E. J. Brill, 1974. An important collection of essays on the religious attitude throughout the late Middle Ages and the Renaissance.

Valdés, Juan de. *Alfabeto Cristiano. Dialogo con Giulia Gonzaga.* Edited by B. Croce. Bari: Gius. Laterza e figli, 1938. Like the *Beneficio*, the *Alfabeto* had enormous diffusion among the Italian *Spirituali*, many of whom were personally acquainted with its author.

_____. *Le cento e dieci divine considerazioni.* Edited by E. Boehmer. Halle: E. Anton, 1860. Very important to the understanding of a thinker who had a great influence on Ochino.

Welti, M. *Kleine Geschichte der italienischen Reformation.* Gütersloh: Gütersloher Verlagshaus, 1985. A short compendium of the history of the Reformation in Italy.

Wicks, J., S.J., ed. and trans. *Cajetan Responds. A Reader in Reformation Controversy.* Washington: The Catholic University of America Press, 1978. An interesting account of an important reaction to the Reformation.

SEVEN DIALOGUES

by the Reverend Father Friar Bernardino Ochino of Siena,
General of the Capuchin Friars, which contain: in the first
one the way in which to grow to love God; in the second
the way in which to achieve happiness; in the third how to
govern oneself; in the fourth the good thief; in the fifth the
pilgrimage to heaven; in the sixth a debate between Christ
and a soul; in the seventh and last one, a profession of faith
with a spiritual testament.

Newly printed and illustrated.

By permission.

1542.

I

A DIALOGUE ABOUT HOW TO GROW TO LOVE GOD[1]

Characters: the Duchess and Friar Bernardino

DUCHESS: Since all that is good derives from God's love, as Christ said in St. Matthew, Ch. XX,[2] all perfection must consist in loving him. For that reason I would be very grateful if you would tell me what to do in order to grow to love my Lord God.

FRIAR BERNARDINO: No one is preoccupied with learning how to love creation. Unfortunately, one simply loves it without needing to be taught. Yet, when it comes to loving God, we are so cold that many of us not only fail to love him, but we also blaspheme him, despise him and hold him in no esteem at all.

DUCHESS: Worse yet, there are many who appear to be incapable of loving him. Yet all that is good comes to us from God. All creation serves us; it is the consequence, the flames, so to speak, of his love. That is why every soul should feed on his love — like a salamander that thrives in the middle of fire.[3]

FRIAR BERNARDINO: Your Grace may now realize the extent of our blindness. Indeed, God possesses all qualities that inspire love to the highest degree. First of all, there is no evil or deficiency in God. On the contrary, there is infinite goodness. As Christ said in St. Matthew, Ch. XIX: "Only God is good,"[4] — that is in essence — and true goodness resides only in him. In creation there is some minimal goodness, but it is not real, it is like a shadow;[5] it depends on divine good-

1

ness, of which it holds a share. In God there is supreme infinite wisdom, beauty, truth, power, mercy, love, charity, and sweetness. Even though sometimes he tries us, he only does it because he loves us. God says: "You have cost me too dear a price. I sent my own Son to die for your sake. I see that you are going to hell and I would rather not lose you. That is why I sometimes send you tribulations to chastise your sensuality." What more can be said? God is all good, he is infinite goodness. All the sweetness, beauty, and goodness to be found in creation are gathered in God, purified of all evil and are supremely perfect. Now Your Grace may understand whether or not one should love him.

DUCHESS: All the more so since loving God is easy. In fact, nothing is as much within our power as to love him. Loving God is also of help to us because, though it is just love, yet it can regain lost grace for us and augment it, so that we ascend to heaven. God does not expect us to shed our blood or give up our lives; he wants our love, and that alone can make us happy. In this life loving God is sweeter and gentler than all other things. It brings one so much honour that it cannot ever be excessive. All other virtues reside in a certain mean or middle course; they lose all excellence if they go beyond it.[6] On the contrary, the more we love God, the better. That is why everyone should love him, place him above everything else, and never desert him, for good or evil, comfort or discomfort, pleasure or displeasure, honour or dishonour. Rather one should say like Paul in his letter to the Romans, Ch. VIII: "Who will separate us from the love of Christ?"[7]

FRIAR BERNARDINO: The three Divine Persons never cease in their intense love of that supreme goodness.[8] The angels and saints ceaselessly love it with perfect love. Even all visible creatures turn with love toward God, in whichever way they can, though they have no rationality. Man, so beloved by God that he created everything for man's sake, being in possession of rationality, should love God above all else. Yet only man perverts the order of love and not only fails to love God above all things but also holds God inferior to the most insignificant creatures. He despises God, holds him in no esteem and mocks him.

DUCHESS: Perhaps the reason is that we cannot love him more than we love ourselves.

FRIAR BERNARDINO: If that were so, then we would be under no obligation.

DUCHESS: Let us examine natural arguments. We naturally tend to love ourselves more intensely than we love everything else. Indeed, all other loves derive from self-love. Since nature cannot be changed, we cannot help loving ourselves more than we love all other things. Equally, we cannot find any creature whose love does not follow nature. No creature loves God naturally, except to the extent that its own existence depends on him. Consequently, a creature will love itself more than it loves God. Let an eagle soar as high as it can. It will never succeed in flying higher than itself, especially if it has no feathers and if it is tied to the ground. In the same way, let a soul rise with love as high as it will. Yet it will never rise above itself so that it will love something else more than it loves itself, especially if it does not have the feathers of moral virtue and if it is tied to lowly things by its own confused desires.

FRIAR BERNARDINO: I am not talking about the natural love which we must feel toward ourselves and all that is comfortable, useful, and pleasurable to us. Nor am I talking about sensual love, through which one cannot approach God, since he cannot be perceived by our senses. Both kinds of love are natural to us and beyond our control. Therefore they can be neither praised nor blamed. I am talking about the free and rational love with which we can love what we want, particularly God, more than we love ourselves, as rationality prompts us to do.[9]

A soul can fly high above itself on the wings of love; it can even grow to love God to such an extent that it will hate and despise itself. A brave citizen can and must give up his own life for the sake of his country. Disregarding every other tie, he must love his own country more than he loves himself. Many citizens determined or vowed to do so, and many did it. All the more, a good Christian can and must risk his life for his heavenly fatherland, or better yet for God, and love God more than himself, as all martyrs and saints have done.

Even great sinners can rise above themselves in this life; they can grow to love God more than they love themselves through divine grace which never fails. In fact, no sinner can be reconciled to God unless his love of God is greater than his own self-love. If that were not possible, then no one in a state of sin would be able to make peace with God and regain his lost grace. Who is there that cannot curb his own natural sensuality for the sake of God's love? Who is there that cannot give up his property, children, pleasures, honours, friends, and titles, or even himself, his own life, his own being, all that he has and will ever have? Even if he cannot do so in actual fact, he can at least wish to do it.

DUCHESS: I find it easy to love creation, but I seem to be unable to love God.

FRIAR BERNARDINO: It is natural and pleasing to our senses to love one's friends and family and all the things from which we derive some use, comfort, delight, or honour. Indeed it is easy to love such things. That is how the wicked love God; not like a father because of his goodness, but like a servant because he is useful and he gives them worldly gifts. That is how a miser loves. There are many others who love him because of the pleasures he gives them — because of their own enjoyment. Such love is lustful. It is the very opposite of sincere, genuine, divine, spiritual, holy love. Others love God because they have received some honour or privilege that they ascribe to him. In a word, all those who love God not because he himself is good, not for his honour and glory, but only because he has granted them something good or because they hope that he will, do not really love God — they love themselves. Since they care only about themselves, they have become their own God. Unable to enjoy having God as their ultimate goal, they think only of themselves, using God as their servant. Such love is not very difficult, but it is not meritorious or virtuous; on the contrary, it is quite sinful.

We must love God above all things, more than we love ourselves, with sincere pure love, only for his honour and glory. Though reason may prompt us to do so, yet our instinctive feelings and desires are not so inclined. They care only for their own gratification; they are averse to perfect love, which renounces everything for God's sake. That love runs against our senses, instincts, and natural desires, which are hardly ever virtuous, meritorious or holy. Because of Adam's sin we have fallen into an immoderate love of material things and into a state of ignorance about divine things. For that reason it is even harder to love God. Yet, though it is not easy to love God more than we love ourselves, it is enough to know that it is within everyone's power through divine grace, which never deserts man.

DUCHESS: So then loving God above all things is not easy but hard?

FRIAR BERNARDINO: It is extremely hard to annihilate oneself for God's sake; indeed, it surpasses everything else in difficulty. That is why perfect love of God deserves so much praise. It is so hard for us that it comprises within itself every other difficulty in the present life. Whoever rises to such a degree of love toward God never experiences any further difficulties in anything else; on the contrary, everything becomes sweet and easy for him. Just as all that is good derives from loving God, so too all that is hard and evil derives from not loving him. Even angels, though they are spiritual substances, found it very hard to love God more than themselves while they were messengers.[10] It is even harder for us. It is easy for the blessed to give God all their love. Also there are many who find it easy in the present life with the great help of divine grace.

DUCHESS: I wish I could love God more than I love creation. Yet I sometimes find that creatures are more enjoyable and sweeter than God.

FRIAR BERNARDINO: God does not expect sweet, but strong, steadfast love from us. He does not expect sensuous, but spiritual love. Love is not based on our likes. On the contrary, one can feel perfect love toward God without any liking at all. Love lies entirely within our power. It does not depend on our likes, which often derive from self-love.

DUCHESS: I love many things in creation, but there are many others that I simply cannot bring myself to love. They just displease me. You may say and do what you like, but loving does not depend on us.

FRIAR BERNARDINO: Sensual love is not in our power. But spiritual love, through which one can love even one's enemies, is entirely voluntary. That being so, who is there that by his actions cannot do good to those who hurt him? Even if he cannot do so in deed, at least in his heart and will he can say to himself: "I would not fail him if I could." The same is true of God. We can all give up everything for Jesus Christ's sake, at least in our hearts, and say: "If I could, I would risk my life for God's love should the occasion arise. For his love, were it necessary, and were it God's will, I would choose to undergo every possible hardship and I would deprive myself of all happiness, if I knew that would please God."

DUCHESS: Now I realize that it is possible for us to grow to love God, even though it is hard. I would like to know what to do to give him all my love.

FRIAR BERNARDINO: Which is the best way according to Your Grace?

DUCHESS: No one can divide himself into two. As Christ said in St. Matthew, Ch. VI: "No one can serve two masters"[11] when they are contrary and opposed to each other. Therefore it is impossible to serve both God and the world with all one's heart. The more love you give the world, the more you take away from God. Whoever wishes to rise to God with all his love must forsake himself and every creature. Indeed, it is impossible to be bound to the world by love and to ascend to God in heaven. A soul that is isolated and nourished by love must necessarily rise up to its creator if it is deprived of every other attraction.

FRIAR BERNARDINO: Our contempt for the world must be born from our love of God, not our love of God from our contempt for the world. First we must love God and then despise the world.

DUCHESS: Yet one reads about many philosophers who despised the world without loving God.

FRIAR BERNARDINO: A wise man must always bear in mind the purpose that prompts him to act. Those who despised the world had some aim in mind.

DUCHESS: Their aim was human praise and glory.

FRIAR BERNARDINO: They were not real philosophers if they were not guided by their love of virtue.

DUCHESS: Many were guided by virtue.

FRIAR BERNARDINO: Then they first loved that virtue or that human glory and they were prompted by their love to despise the world. Just so must a good Christian be prompted to despise everything by his love of Jesus Christ. He must learn to hate himself because of his love of God, since hate always derives from love, not love from hate. Of course, it is true that one could despise the world even without loving God, if one only stopped to consider that the world is next to nothing when compared to God. There is no goodness in it and it is full of all evils. Whoever did that would quickly grow to love God. This is the first way to grow to love God, in respect of God himself. Now I would like Your Grace to tell me what else you think one should do.

DUCHESS: One can love something one has never seen,[12] but only if one acquires some knowledge of it. But it is impossible to love something we do not know. In that respect the intellect serves the will, his queen.[13] He precedes her carrying a lamp. It is impossible for the will to apply herself to anything unless the intellect first becomes acquainted with it.

Therefore, whoever ascends to God must first reach the cherubim and then the seraphim. In other words, he must be first cherubic and then seraphic. First he must gain some understanding and knowledge of God, and then he must love him.[14] In the heavenly hierarchy the Holy Spirit presupposes the Son of God; equally, love presupposes knowledge.[15] That means that we can only love what we know. The more one understands the goodness of something, the more one loves it.

This may be proved from experience. If one sees a man from a distance, one does not love him very much because one does not know him well. The same happens if one sees his shadow or image. When one sees the man from a closer distance, one loves him more. When one finally gets to know him, one realizes his virtues which shine from the goodness of his life and one loves him all the more. One loves goodness the better one knows it. I think that may be the reason God is not loved very much. We have a scant understanding of God and we only care for, think about, and concern ourselves with things relating to this life.

Also, as Paul wrote in his first letter to the Corinthians, Ch. VIII: "We see God as an enigma, imperfectly and through the mirror of creation, which is dim for us." He also wrote this in his letter to the Romans, Ch. I.[16] We are like night moths that cannot bear to look at the sunlight.[17] God is infinite, immense, and uncircumscribed; our minds are finite and limited. They

8

are locked in the dark prisons of our bodies, tainted by original sin, and often also by their own malice which blinds them. In such darkness we only see God imperfectly. As is written, he dwells in inaccessible light. He is clad in splendour and has shrouded his hiding-place in darkness.[18] One can realize from experience that God is little loved because he is little known. The three Divine Persons have perfect infinite knowledge of God's divine essence. Therefore they love him with infinite love, which is commensurate with his infinite light.[19] The blessed love God perfectly because they dwell in his clear day and they can see him by noonlight. Whoever can see his infinite goodness more clearly, loves him more. On the contrary, the poor damned souls do not love him because they are plunged in darkest night and deprived of God's living light. We are in darkness and have an imperfect knowledge of God, though we do partially know him, as Paul wrote in his first letter to the Corinthians, Ch. XIII.[20] That is why we do not love him very much.

We could have had better knowledge of him in earthly paradise. There we could have loved him more. However, since we now are closer to hell than to heaven, we know him very little and also love him very little. Those who had a better knowledge of God during their lives loved him more, for instance, the Virgin Mary, Paul, the Apostles, Augustine, Jerome, Ambrose, Gregory, Francis, and others. We instead do not love him much because we put little effort into getting to know him. We only care for the world. That is all we enjoy, talk, or think about. No one studies Scripture or Christ's life. People have forgotten God, his love and his many benefits. They have lost their faith. They live for the present, as if there were no other life except this one. That is why one finds so little love of God. However, according to me, the best way to grow to love God would be for people to make an effort to know him and to take time to meditate about him.

FRIAR BERNARDINO: Which of God's attributes should one meditate about?

DUCHESS: That God is singular, eternal, necessary, infinite, immense, limitless, and uncircumscribed. One should meditate upon the fact that the Father is ungenerated; that by means of his fecund memory he generates the Son, to whom he communicates all his perfection, though all of it still remains in the Father.[21] One should also meditate about the way in which the Father and the Son spirate[22] and bring forth the Holy Spirit by means of their fecund will; about how they communicate their perfection to it, without they themselves losing any of it. One should also consider the way in which the three Divine Persons are identical in essence, though they are personally distinguished by their individual attributes, whether they are considered in an absolute or an individual sense.[23] One should also meditate upon the identity, similarity, and equality among the three Divine Persons; the ideas in God's mind and what they are; how it is possible for God to foresee future contingent events from eternity with certain infallible knowledge, and yet also to depend on our free will, so that we are free; and how, though God has foreordained everything from eternity, he remains immutable in his decisions.[24] If one considered such things when meditating about God, one would necessarily become inflamed with divine love.

FRIAR BERNARDINO: If things were as Your Grace has described them, only the learned could love God. Yet I believe that a simple little old woman can love God as much as the greatest sage in the world.[25] To have that kind of knowledge about God does not help one to love him. Those are called speculations and they are rather a hindrance. When the soul becomes involved in such sublimities it loses sight of love; it remains barren and cold, just like the wise men of this world. Writing about them to the Romans, in Ch. I, Paul said that though they had some speculative knowledge of God, yet they did not glorify him or thank him as

God. Their thoughts remained vain and their foolish hearts grew dark.[26] Lucifer himself had a profound understanding of God. It is written in Ezechiel, Ch. XXVIII, that he was full of wisdom,[27] yet he did not turn to God with love. What good is it to speculate about every possible aspect of God and not to love him?

It is wrong for us to seek to understand certain strange unusual things about God which do not help to love him. They call that speculative knowledge and it serves to understand. Yet it is practical knowledge that leads you to love: for instance, thinking that God is supreme goodness, that he loves us and takes care of us, and that he let his Son be crucified for our sake. It is useful to reflect on such things in order to grow to love God. Such knowledge may easily be acquired even by the simple and unlearned, to whom the kingdom of heaven belongs, as Christ said in St. Matthew, Ch. III.[28] Too much knowledge and subtle speculation hinder our love of God. That is why David said in his Psalm: "Because I had no knowledge and I was not illuminated by learning, I will enter through the Lord's gate and into the prophesied sacred stigmata of Christ."[29] Whoever wishes to rise toward God's perfect love must avoid all vain, useless, strange doctrines, as Paul exhorts us to do in his letter to Titus, Ch. III.[30] He must seek to know only those things that inflame one with divine love. Our Jesus Christ.[31]

DUCHESS: I beg you, please tell me which things inspire us with divine love when we have knowledge of them?

FRIAR BERNARDINO: First of all, one must look at creation, not only to despise it because it is nothing compared to God. One must also consider the way in which divine goodness, wisdom, power, beauty, love, and the other divine attributes shine in it as in a mirror, so that they may be known through creation, as is written in Romans, Ch. I.[32] Perceiving the beauty of creation, Your Grace should not stop there. You should be inspired by it to rise and to ascend to divine beauty,

11

while thinking that all this beauty is nothing by comparison with God's beauty. One must use creation like a ladder by which to rise to divine beauty. One must ascend to heaven in one's thoughts, saying to oneself: "If one can find so much sweetness in creation, which really is like a muddy brook sprinkled with a lot of bitterness, what will it be like to enjoy that infinite sea of love? What will it be like to see oneself mirrored in that divine wisdom with which he could rule infinite worlds, seeing that he amazes us by the way in which he rules even this world alone?"

How great is God's tireless power and might! With it he created the universe out of nothing and he preserves it; with it he could all of a sudden create and annihilate an infinite number of worlds![33] God's goodness, mercy, clemency, and sweetness are great indeed. Foreseeing our great sins, he not only waits for us, but he always calls us to repent, and forgives our every mistake unless we are indifferent. Who could express even a thousandth part of the love Jesus Christ, our Lord, has shown us and continually shows us? Like a good father, not only did he create us, but he also preserves and guides us. He takes special care of us and he serves us through all creation. Meditating on divine perfection is very helpful in growing to love God. Sometimes we ought to think about the beauty and variety of all the different flowers and fruits, pearls, jewels and precious gems, gold, silver, and all the other lowly things in creation. Then we should rise to the contemplation of the light of the stars, sun, and other celestial bodies. Next we should consider the beauty of the human soul, especially when it is clad in virtue and enriched by spiritual gifts, understanding, and grace. Then we should turn the mind's eyes toward the blissful angelic spirits, beginning from the angels, then rising to the archangels, and so on from rank to rank right up to the seraphim. If we could only cast a fleeting glance at the Mother of God and see her beauty, it would be an adequate reward for all our troubles. We would be more than repaid. If those who saw her here on earth could be considered happy, Your Grace may imagine what it would be like to see her in heaven. If our living thoughts could only rise, not to Christ's divinity, but just to his gracious humanity; if we could see his sacred stigmata and understand his great love; if we could see his loving, blissful, divine face, which even the angels long to contemplate; then we could consider ourselves truly happy. Yet the beauty, sweetness, goodness, love, and perfection of all those things is nothing by comparison with God. Divine perfection infinitely exceeds all creation, without comparison.

DUCHESS: Can one in any other way reach such knowledge of God that it will prompt one to love him?

FRIAR BERNARDINO: No doubt, and a more perfect way.

DUCHESS: What is it?

FRIAR BERNARDINO: Reading books. I do not mean poets, historians, philosophers, and books relating to what happens in this world. What I mean is Scripture, the lives of the saints, their deeds, their actions, their profound ardour, their wise, inflamed, holy words. Their books still contain sparks of the fire and zeal that animated them. If we read them, we will necessarily burn with love. That is why the prophet said: "The fire of divine love will be lit in my meditation."[34] If books written by people now dead can so inflame us, how much more can that be achieved by those who are alive? How good it is to hear the words of one who is burning with divine love in order to grow to love God! Just as a burning piece of iron taken out of a furnace casts sparks all around, so too one whose heart is aglow with God's love must sparkle with love through all his senses. Words coming from the heart are like burning flames that inflame the people who hear them. Living examples are much more compelling than words. That is why talking with those who are holy and perfect is a great help in growing to love God.[35]

DUCHESS: I think meditating about Christ's life and words is more useful than anything else in order to reach perfect knowledge of God's goodness and divine perfection, and to grow to love him. As Christ himself said in St. John, Ch. X, he is the door through which one reaches divine love.[36]

FRIAR BERNARDINO: Although God showed us in the creation and preservation of the world a glimmer of his power, goodness, justice, mercy, wisdom, and other attributes, yet he also took on human flesh. With profound humility he uttered kind words and showed man his loving feelings, sweetly dealing and conversing with man for thirty-three years. He showed us the way to heaven. He underwent a cruel, shameful death for our sake. In that was seen not only a spark, but an infinite sea of God's goodness, mercy, and love. That is why, through Christ, a simple Christian can obtain an understanding of God and his perfection a thousand times better than that which all the philosophers and sages of this world can obtain through creation.

We should all let go of creation and let our hearts say to the world: "I am leaving you to go to Jesus Christ." Just as it is impossible for fire to burn in water, so is it impossible for divine love to burn in a worldly heart. Whoever wishes to go to Jesus Christ must forsake himself and everything else. We must gather our thoughts and energy, which have so far been diverted by creation, and place them all in God. We must say to ourselves: "I have served the world long enough. After all, I am God's child and I am bound to love him for many different reasons. Oh vile world, I have served you all my life and you have always cheated me! Oh my stinking body, which very soon will be nothing but a rotten bag of worms, until now I have taken care of you and I have done nothing for the soul, your sister.[37] If she is damned, you will be damned too. It is better to change my life and habits. Come on, let us cast aside all vanity, riches, pleasures, and honours. From now on I will only talk about God.

I have talked about the world long enough. I will only hear, taste, smell, and think about God. In fact, I will always keep my eyes fixed upon him."

DUCHESS: Which of Christ's qualities should we meditate about in order to understand God and to give him all our love?

FRIAR BERNARDINO: His profound humility, his deep sublime wisdom, his extreme poverty, his unending patience, his humble obedience, his boundless love, his sweet compassion, his cruel penance, vigils and abstinence, his fervent prayers and his other qualities. They can be contemplated through his words, actions and virtues. If a soul longed for Christ like a true bride, if her eyes could meet his and if, even in part, she could taste his love and all that he suffered for her sake, if she could see his burning tears, hear the deep ardent sighs coming from his inflamed heart, see his loving blood and realize his thirst for her salvation, then she could not help loving him. Or else, if she reviewed all of Christ's life in her mind, from the time when he was conceived until the moment when he ascended to heaven; if she could gather in the closet of her memory[38] all his words, tears and sighs, his fasting, abstinence, pilgrimages and prayers, the blame, insults, persecutions, scourgings, beatings and blows that he endured, the sadness in his heart and all his love; then she could not help becoming inflamed with divine love. What need is there for any more words? All that Christ suffered and endured was only for our sake.

Oh how blind, cold, obstinate, and hard-hearted you are not to burn constantly with divine love, when the whole world is aflame! All creatures serve man and they are like flames! Fire kindles fire better than anything else does. Love generates love. Let Your Grace consider God's numberless benefits, favours, and gifts. Imagine how many more he would have granted us if we had not rebelled. The Eternal Father gave us his own incarnated Son as an example, a light, a mirror, a ransom, as food, life, death, and in every possible way in which he could give him to us. He will give him to us again as a reward. As Paul said: "In giving us such a precious thing, he necessarily gave us all."[39] He gave us the Holy Spirit and he gave himself to us. If, with clear understanding, one meditated not only about such benefits, but also about the infinite love with which they were given, then one's soul would feel so much sweetness that it could not help but detach itself from the body and ascend to God. But we seldom think about it and then only superficially.

DUCHESS: Above all else, I think it is useful to have perfect faith in God's love and his benefits. If we truly believed that God loves us with infinite, constant, sincere, and gratuitous love; that he only acts for our sake; that he let his Son be crucified for us, and that any good derives from him; then we would have to love him. But we seldom think about it, much less do we believe it. It is enough if we just pay lip-service to this truth from time to time.

FRIAR BERNARDINO: Your Grace has found the root of all our evils. I think that we love to the extent to which we believe. Since we do not believe very much, we cannot love very much either.

DUCHESS: Besides God's love, tell me what else is there about God that a gentle soul could meditate on; what else could help us to give all our love to God?

FRIAR BERNARDINO: One should meditate about his goodness, justice, mercy, sweetness, and mildness; his wisdom, beauty, truth, and power, and similar divine attributes, avoiding the thought of their infinitude. One must always avoid dwelling on any subtle idle[40] questions; avoid those things which do not prompt the love of God, but rather confuse it. One must imitate a child sucking his mother's milk: he hugs her close and thinks of nothing except enjoying that milk. He does not stop to wonder whether it is white or black, warm or cold; he is all intent on enjoying it. So too the soul must entirely forget itself and all those things in God which do not help us to love him. It must concentrate on loving him or reflecting on things that inflame it with love.

DUCHESS: Is there anything else in God that may help us to get to love him, besides his love and perfection?

FRIAR BERNARDINO: His very being is the infinite source, the sea and fountain from which all divine perfection flows and in which all goodness is rooted.

DUCHESS: Many have said that though one must understand and get to know creation before one can get to love it, it is quite different with God. On the contrary, he cannot be perfectly understood except through love. That is why the prophet said: "Taste and see."[41] Through love one tastes his great sweetness even before getting to know it. Since God is not commensurate to human intellect, he cannot be perfectly understood unless man's will first tries to reach God with perfect love, and becoming identified with him, begins to glow with love. Then the intellect, inflamed by the transformation of the soul, becomes capable of understanding God perfectly. Since grace first descends on the seraphim and through them on the cherubim, man's will must first be seraphic. Then the intellect will mortify itself and become cherubic.[42] Just as, when ascending, one first reaches the Holy Spirit, the third of the Divine Persons, before reaching the Son of God, so the mind rising toward God reaches love before knowledge.[43]

Indeed worldly love blinds us; divine love illuminates us and enables us to understand divine goodness, which cannot be perfectly known in any other way. The more we love, the more we taste and know; the more we know, the more we love. Therefore love helps to reach perfect knowledge and knowledge increases love. According to this view on how to reach perfect love, one must not only forget all creation, but one must also forget oneself and all the subtle questions about God discussed by the wise men of this world. One must also forget God's divine love and divine perfection, and everything else. Not allowing one's mind to dwell on anything, one must direct all one's faculties to love. A blind man with a keen sense of taste applies all his concentration to tasting the sweetness of honey. He perceives it perfectly, much better than all those whose eyesight is good but whose palate is spoiled. Just so, the simple soul which offers itself up entirely to God perceives him and tastes him better than all the enlightened thinkers in the world.

FRIAR BERNARDINO: It is quite true that God can inspire love in the human will even if the intellect has no knowledge of the object of that love. But it is not possible for the will to act on the basis of such love. It is also not possible for the will to generate such love even as a secondary and partial cause, unless the intellect has knowledge of it. Therefore some knowledge is necessary before one can grow to love God. Yet it is true, as I have already said, that in order to reach that love we must only try to understand those things that serve it and we must become all absorbed in God's love. God's love illuminates us and by this experience leads us to know God's goodness, sweetness, charity, wisdom, and his other virtues. We will know them much better if we taste them than if we learn about them in theory.

DUCHESS: I would like to know if tasting God's sweetness is a help in loving him.

FRIAR BERNARDINO: To enjoy God is not the same as to love him. We do not always love the things that we enjoy. Since our likes derive from self-love, a soul seeking them is not God's bride, but rather a harlot. One may derive enjoyment from God while at the same time being guilty of every possible mortal sin. God grants enjoyment to the imperfect in the same way that one gives milk to lambs because they cannot eat solid food, as is said in Hebrews, Ch. V,[44] or as one waters new plants that have not yet taken root perfectly. Who would not be willing to give up the world's sweetness for that of Christ? But the point is that one should give up the world for the insults, shame, persecution, poverty, abstinence, and cross of Christ. How many there are who think that they are looking for Jesus Christ when they are only looking for themselves, seeking their own likes, enjoyments and pleasures! True love of God makes one ignore pleasure or displeasure, praise or blame, personal good or evil, and makes one care only for God's glory. Whoever really loves God is not troubled when he feels no enjoyment. He considers himself unworthy of any happiness, but that does not stop him from loving God. On the contrary, he takes advantage of this opportunity to love him better, thinking that God deprives him of any enjoyment so that he may love God more perfectly. If he happens to feel any enjoyment, he humbles himself saying: "God gives me some enjoyment because I am imperfect, so that I may not fail on my way to him. I am fed milk like a little child because of my imperfection." It becomes a reason for him to love God more intensely, thinking about how great divine goodness really is. Though he is imperfect, yet God does not fail to help him in every possible way.

DUCHESS: Everything is clear now. Talking often inspires me.

FRIAR BERNARDINO: In the Acts of the Apostles, Ch. II, the Holy Spirit descends in tongues of fire[45] and in the last chapter of St. Luke, the two disciples who were going to Emmaus say: "Did our hearts not burn when he spoke to us on the way?"[46] In Hebrews, Ch. X: "God's word is alive and effective; it pierces people's hearts and inflames them."[47]

DUCHESS: Thinking about Jesus Christ and all that he endured for my sake is much more useful to me.

FRIAR BERNARDINO: Christ came from heaven to earth to bring fire. He only wants it to burn, as he himself said.[48] He could have healed and redeemed mankind without suffering. Yet to show us his great love, which shines nowhere more clearly than in his suffering, he chose to die so that his love would compel us to love him.

DUCHESS: I wish I could love him above all things. Yet I do not love him as much as I should.

FRIAR BERNARDINO: Whoever truly wishes to love him, loves him very much. But the point is that we are tepid in our wish to love him and so we do not love him enough.

DUCHESS: Is it not enough for me to wish that I could will myself to love him?

FRIAR BERNARDINO: Indeed it is, provided that your wish is strong enough. We are deceived by the beauty and sweetness of the things of this world. Let us rather conceive in our minds an image of all the beauty, mildness, and goodness of our Creator. By contemplating not creation, but beauty and goodness in themselves, we will grow blind to all lowly things. Such love is Moses' burning bush, Elijah's fiery chariot, the parted tongues of fire.[49] Only in God's love can we find peace and a blissful haven for our wishes, a true rest after our labours, a sure remedy for our sorrows, and the best cure for all evils.

May Your Grace engage in such spiritual exercises, annihilating yourself by becoming identified with God. May that be granted to you by him who was crucified for our sake.

Alleluia.

The end.

II

A DIALOGUE ABOUT HOW TO ACHIEVE HAPPINESS

Characters: Friar Bernardino and the Duchess of Camerino

Friar Bernardino asks and the Duchess answers.

FRIAR BERNARDINO *(aside)*: I can see that Her Grace the Duchess looks very dejected and tired. According to me she must be looking for something very important. I will be bold and ask her what she hopes to achieve by all her preoccupations. — Please, I beg Your Grace to deign to tell me what you are looking for in this world with so much eagerness, torment, and suffering.

DUCHESS: I am looking for some peace and quiet but I cannot find them.

FRIAR BERNARDINO: How long have you been looking for them?

DUCHESS: For all my life I have fought only to be at peace; I have endured misery to no longer be miserable; I have been in perennial motion to achieve stillness and yet I have not found it for even a single hour. When looking for happiness in this world, I have only found misery. So I think that happiness cannot be found during this life.

FRIAR BERNARDINO: Of course, not the happiness the blessed enjoy in heaven. Yet one can find the kind of happiness that is suited to our present state. Indeed, man would be too miserable if no remedy could be found for his unhappiness.

21

DUCHESS: Then you think that one can find happiness in this world?

FRIAR BERNARDINO: Of course I do not think that this world can make us entirely happy. Yet I am quite sure that it is possible for a human being to find the sort of happiness in this life which is suited to pilgrims.

DUCHESS: Surely that cannot apply to everyone.

FRIAR BERNARDINO: Everyone can be happy if he so wishes.

DUCHESS: I do not think so.

FRIAR BERNARDINO: Why not?

DUCHESS: Because in that case everyone would want to be happy. That is our first and supreme wish. If it lay in our power, then everyone would be able to find happiness and to ultimately attain it.

FRIAR BERNARDINO: Perhaps they are not looking for it in the right way.

DUCHESS: Perhaps finding it takes a very long time.

FRIAR BERNARDINO: On the contrary, happiness can be found immediately by everyone.

DUCHESS: That means that I could be happy today if I wished.

FRIAR BERNARDINO: Without a doubt.

DUCHESS: Please tell me what to do. If I know how to do it and if I can do it, I will do my utmost to be happy.

FRIAR BERNARDINO: On the contrary, I am afraid you will not.

DUCHESS: Do you think that I will contradict myself, that I will prevent my own happiness and become an enemy to my own well-being?

FRIAR BERNARDINO: That is precisely what I fear.

DUCHESS: It is impossible that I should so much wish to be happy and not do what is necessary, if it lies within my power.

FRIAR BERNARDINO: You will have to decide if happiness is in Your Grace's power, if it is in your duchy of Camerino or if it lies in your own words. As Christ said in St. Luke, Ch. XVII, "The kingdom of God lies within yourselves."[1] Perhaps you still have long way to go.

DUCHESS: Yet I have looked for happiness everywhere I could and I have never found it.

FRIAR BERNARDINO: Perhaps you have not looked for it where it really is.

DUCHESS: I have looked for it where I thought it might be.

FRIAR BERNARDINO: And where was that?

DUCHESS: In health, wealth, my state, rule, and power. I have looked for it in pomp and vanity, in pampering my own body with all comforts, in exquisite, varied, elaborate foods, in jewels, clothes and ornaments. I have looked for it in honour, praise and dignity, in the pleasures and sensual delights of the world. I have looked for it in my family and friends, in endearing myself to all. I have looked for it in learning and rhetoric, in the moral virtues, in speculating about truth, in the contemplation of God, in the enjoyment of everything, above all, of God. In a word, I have experienced everything and I have found misery where I thought there was happiness.

FRIAR BERNARDINO: I am not surprised that you have never found it. You have not looked for it where it really is.

DUCHESS: Yet I have looked for it in all things.

FRIAR BERNARDINO: Happiness lies within ourselves. One must not wander outside oneself in order to find it. Even if there were an infinite number of worlds,[2] they could not fully satisfy a soul. Its capacity is too great. Nothing below God can ever satisfy a soul, because it is capable of containing God. An apple, a spherical body, could not fill up a triangular vase; the corners would always remain empty. The soul was created in the image of the Trinity and it cannot be filled by the earth, which is round. The soul's intellect, memory, and will are always bound to remain empty.[3] Only God and the almighty Trinity are similar to the soul and can fill it up.

So long as our minds wander from one creature to another, we pass from one desire to another and we never stop. That happens because we can never find anything so perfect in the world that our desire cannot exceed it. On the contrary, our desire transcends all creatures and goes beyond them all the way to God. There it stops because a man cannot rise further to anything more perfect, either by thought or desire. Whoever thinks that he will find perfect satisfaction in creation is like one who thinks that he will quench his thirst by eating salt. The more of this world we have, the more we would like to have. Creation does not soothe or satisfy our desires; instead, it excites and awakens them. Those who have the most, desire the most. It must be said that such people are the poorest ones, since desire derives from indigence and poverty. It is not those who have the most that are happy, but those who desire the least. It is your heart that you must fill, not your coffers.

The wheel of the world keeps turning without ever stopping. Whoever is tied to it with the chains of love and the ropes of desire must turn all the time and be in perennial motion. One must detach one's love from the world and stop desiring the things in creation. Then let the wheel turn whichever way it likes! We will just mock it! Whoever does not love or desire is free from sadness, perturbation, fear or anxiety. He never feels miserable. On the contrary, he can laugh at everything. Those who wish to put an end to their own unhappiness must put an end to their desires. As Crates said: "We must not augment our honours, riches and pleasures, but diminish our greed."[4] As Seneca says: "No one can have everything, but it is in everyone's power to despise everything; therefore it is easy for all of us to be happy not by having, but by despising."[5] Whoever wishes to be happy must not tie himself with love to frail, fleeting, transitory things, but to eternal, stable ones which cannot be lost. That is why Plato said that a man is happy only when he depends on God.[6] Our greed is boundless and it always longs for new things. For that reason the gymnosophists said that happiness consists in giving up everything and depriving oneself of all things.[7] Those who are poorest in desire are richest in happiness for, as Cleanthes said, they are in possession of themselves.[8]

DUCHESS: As you say, nearly everyone deceives himself by thinking that he will fill the insatiable abyss of his own desires by hoarding. They increase their own misery while thinking that they will find happiness.

FRIAR BERNARDINO: Let whoever wishes to quench his own thirst forever, go to the source where all fresh, pure, limpid, clear, and infinite waters are merged and gathered.

The end.

Praise be to God.

Although just as a river brings him gold,
A miser hoards wealth in abundancy,
And lots of good and fruitful land does hold,
And gems and pearls all gathered from the sea.
What benefit or profit can these hold,
If they will never sate his fond fancy?
His worry never passes while he lives,
And when he dies all riches up he gives.[9]

III

A DIALOGUE ABOUT
HOW A MAN SHOULD
BEST GOVERN HIMSELF

Characters: Master and Pupil

MASTER: I do not think there is anything in the world more necessary to man than to know how to govern and control oneself well. Just as all motion depends on that of the First Mover,[1] so all control depends on self-control. No one can govern an empire, a kingdom, a province, a city or a family well unless he can first govern himself. It is impossible to straighten up one's own shadow if one is bent over. It is also impossible to correct others unless one corrects oneself. As is written, whoever is not good to himself cannot be good to others. What can be worse than not knowing how to live virtuously?

PUPIL: I would like to know how a man should govern himself so that he may follow the best possible course all his life.

MASTER: Except for rational beings, all other creatures follow a pattern in their actions. They let themselves be ruled by God.[2] Therefore they reach the goals intended for them. But man, since he is free, often resists divine inspiration. As if he were a god on earth, he prefers to govern himself, deviating from divine will. As a result, all his life is in a state of utter confusion, though it should be better ordered than the lives of other creatures because of his intelligence. There are very few who know how to govern themselves and even fewer who are willing to learn. Nearly all of us think we are great masters in that art.

Yet to err in directing one's own life is the greatest error of all. Whoever misses his way loses his soul, heaven, and everything else. First of all, everyone ought to take care of himself. Real happiness (as Cleanthes said)[3] consists in being one's own master; in controlling and governing oneself. Whoever achieves that is a real king. Conversely, the greatest misery that can happen in this life is not to know how to govern oneself and to become a slave and a servant to one's own passions. Such a man does not deserve to be free or to be called a man. That is why Plato wrote in his book of wisdom[4] that no art is nobler and more necessary to us than the art of knowing how to live virtuously. Equally, nothing is more depraved and harmful than a state of dissonance and inner discord in the kingdom of our soul.

God does not concern himself with the world[5] until the generation of the three Divine Persons within is completed.[6] Equally, we ought to have nothing to do with governing the world until we are inwardly perfect. Many people are like my steward, who tries hard to keep my household in order but hardly ever takes care of his own house. We are more interested in governing others than in governing ourselves. How many there are who are wise, useful, and honourable to others, but not to themselves! They take good care of their states, families, and fellow-beings, or of their own bodies, but they pay no attention to their own souls. Yet nothing should make us feel more ashamed than not knowing how to live virtuously and to govern ourselves. Real triumph and true victory consist in self-control. Real rule resides in mastering our own passions and real power lies in governing ourselves. Therefore I would like to examine the way in which a man should best be guided.

PUPIL: I must confess that I am not very good at it. Therefore I enjoy talking about it in order to learn — especially with one who knows.

MASTER: A man's soul is like a kingdom in which the will is the queen.[7] Her duty ought to be that of governing herself well, subduing all the other powers of the soul and directing them toward God, by following what is good and hating what is evil. Yet her freedom enables her to do as she likes. She is blind: she cannot see nor is she capable of seeing. That is why God has placed a great sage beside her called the intellect, so that she may be guided by his judgment. But he is also her subject, and he has to consider now one thing, now another one, according to her wishes.[8]

PUPIL: I should like to know about all his different duties.

MASTER: The intellect is illuminated by the light of natural understanding[9] and he sees what is needed for the proper guidance of the soul. Often he sees because he is illuminated by acquired or divinely inspired supernatural knowledge.[10] Turning to the will he tells her all that she must do, commanding all that is necessary for her salvation. He also forbids her to do those things which prevent one from ascending to God. He persuades her to do things which are useful but not indispensable, such as to follow evangelical counsels.[11] He dissuades her from doing useless things and he keeps urging her to do what is good and discouraging her from doing evil. If she acts according to his suggestions, he praises her, applauds her, and gives signs of joy, saying: "How wise you were to obey me!". If she does the opposite, he rails at her, reviles her, grumbles and complains. What more can one say? Reason and the intellect are like the rudder of a ship, with which one steers her and guides her into the harbour. In the same way, reason guides one to heaven.

Furthermore I want you to know that the intellect keeps two books: in one of them he writes down all our good deeds, in the other one all our evil deeds.

Those two books will be opened on the day of judgment and we will be judged according to them. The two books are entrusted to memory, which acts as a treasurer in charge of all the wealth of our knowledge and stores all the appearances and images of the things that the intellect apprehends. In this kingdom there are also ladies-in-waiting, such as the cognitive capacity, the imagination, the estimative capacity and the fantasy.[12] They all serve the intellect; therefore they ultimately serve the will. It is their duty to interpret the appearances of the things that come in through the windows of the senses, so that the appearances can meet the intellect, which is all pure and spiritual. There is also a steward, common sense, who takes care of all strangers, that is, of all the things that come in through the doors of our five senses. Then there are also our five external senses, that is sight, hearing, taste, smell, and touch which, like nuncios and ambassadors of the soul, bring in all the information from the outside and are subject to the will.

PUPIL: I think it must be hard to rule this kingdom well. All the virtues and natural powers of the soul, including the will, thirst naturally and with intense desire after things which are convenient, useful, pleasurable, and honourable to them. They pay no attention to what is right or honest. They are like wild horses, unless they are curbed by the bridle of reason. It is very hard to keep such unrestrained powers under control. They are corrupted, tainted and infected by original sin; they are also poorly trained. Not only does the will naturally love the things of this world; it is also led to them by all the senses, whose pleasures it naturally shares, though she is free to resist. On the one hand, we are in the middle of material things. They surround us on every side and offer themselves to our senses, moving them and exciting them to experience pleasure. On the other hand, divine things are very remote from us and the intellect has little understanding of them. We do not see them, feel them or enjoy them as intensely as we do ordinary things. Yet even if we did enjoy them, God should not be loved because he is sweet and does what is good for us, but for his honour and glory.

MASTER: There is no doubt that it is extremely hard to be an excellent king to oneself. It is not a task for cowards, but for lofty, generous, great spirits.

PUPIL: Which is the first requisite in order to govern oneself?

MASTER: We have to know our own aims. Our intellect must realize and understand that God is our ultimate goal. That is why he preserves us and he has created us. That is why he has redeemed us and ordained everything so that we may ascend to him. Therefore all one's life must be ordered around him; all our love, actions, thoughts and wishes must tend toward him. Man must not live aimlessly. Like a true sage, he must keep his ultimate goal in mind, saying: "This is my goal, this is what I must attain."

PUPIL: There are many who are so blind that they think God has created them so that they may eat and be merry in this life. They think that is their ultimate aim. Let us leave them aside and return to our previous topic. What else is required?

MASTER: The second necessary thing is that the intellect should turn to the will, after finding his ultimate goal, and say: "I have found a great treasure. I have found the ultimate aim for which God created us and placed us in this world. I have found our real fatherland, our kingdom, father, friends, treasures, real honours and pleasures, and our highest and most perfect happiness."

Third, the will must ask the intellect: "What is this goal of ours? In order to inspire me with the wish to ascend toward it, I command you and desire you to inquire in detail into all its attributes and qualities, so that they will excite and inflame me with the wish to reach it. Then you must come and tell me, but first make sure that you know all about them."

Fourth, the intellect obeys the will. He looks for all those things in God which may move the will to love him.

Fifth, he reports to the will, saying: "I have found that God is our ultimate aim. He is supremely good, beautiful, sweet, mild, loving, merciful, just, truthful, omnipotent, and wise. I find that he has always loved us, he loves us, and he will love us with supreme, infinite, eternal, continuous, gratuitous, sincere, pure love and that he holds every perfection in himself. I find that he is your true, legitimate bridegroom. For your sake he created the world and only for you he sent his Son on earth. For you he suffered for thirty-three years and shed his blood on the cross. For you he has prepared heaven and he awaits you there."

Sixth, the will is amazed at the supreme excellence of her goal, at so much goodness and infinite love. She says to the intellect: "Find out if it is at all possible for me to reach my goal, and do your best to lead me to him."

Seventh, the intellect considers our strength, divine grace and all the other things which help us to ascend to God. He realizes that it is possible for the soul to achieve perfect union with God.

Eighth, he says to the will: "Though our own powers are all scarce and weak, yet God makes up for it with divine grace which never fails. Provided you are willing and try hard, you will be able to ascend to God and to find happiness there."

Ninth, the will must express her acceptance of her ultimate goal, saying: "If that is so, then I want him and I accept him as my supreme good. I will direct all my actions, thoughts, love, and all my life toward him."

Tenth, turning to the intellect, she commands him to look for all the necessary and useful means to reach that goal and to explain them to her. He must also show her all the harmful things that may hinder her or hurt her on her way to God, so that she will be on her guard, escape them, and avoid them. He is to pay no attention to indifferent things.

Eleventh, the intellect has to obey. He examines every possible way that he can find to rise to God. He says: "Perhaps it would be good to be a merchant in order to be saved," and he examines that possibility. Realizing all its dangers, he says: "I might easily die.[13] It would probably be better to be a priest, but perhaps not, because I might easily get caught in the snare of my own benefices.[14] Belonging to a monastic order might be a better way, but perhaps if I placed such a heavy noose around my own neck I would not be able to endure it."[15] So he examines all the ways in which God may be reached.

Twelfth, after examining every possibility, he reaches his conclusion and says: "I think it better to follow this way rather than the other ones."

Thirteenth, he reports to the will, saying: "I have examined everything and I cannot find a better way to reach God than this one."

Fourteenth, the will says: "Since I do not trust you too much, I wish you, and also command you, to seek the advice of others, the better to understand and know which way is the best, shortest, safest, and most pleasing to God. Look for wise persons who are instructed in divine things. They must be good and love virtuous living so as to be willing and able to give you proper advice. Also, consider very well the way that saints have followed. Let them be your mirrors, particularly Christ, who was the light, way, guide, mirror, law, rule, and example of all virtue for everyone. He is the book from which one learns to live well. Examine carefully, in Scripture and in every possible way, the ways of that living king, who is most pleasing to God and most perfect in himself. Make sure that you examine everything well, for living virtuously is a vital matter. One must fulfil every requisite. It is enough for one requisite to be missing and everything will be ruined. Anyone can grope his way to hell, but in order to go to heaven one must see the light really well."

Fifteenth, the intellect obeys her in everything. Through reasoning he tries in every way to learn the best ways in which one can be saved.

Sixteenth, he says to the will: "I have found that the way of God's love is safer, shorter, clearer, easier, and more virtuous than all the rest. Besides, one cannot reach him in any other way. You walk in proportion as you love God and no more. This is the way which the saints followed and this is the way shown by the loving Jesus in his own life and teaching. This way is pleasing to divine will, who is the empress, queen, and mother of all created wills who have to obey her."

Seventeenth, the will says: "If that is so, I will love God with all my strength. I no longer wish to live according to the false opinions of the crowd, but according to the dictates of reason, which I will not be ashamed to obey. I will no longer precede the intellect but follow him and hold him as my guide." So the will must choose according to the suggestions of the intellect. She must make her choice at once and not say: "I will start tomorrow." after reaching the right decision, as many people do.

Eighteenth, after the will has chosen to love God, she commands the intellect to consider all those things which are apt to incite her to rise toward perfect love of God.

Nineteenth, the intellect obeys and looks for every possible way, action, and means by which the will may reach supreme love of God and ascend to him.

Twentieth, the intellect says to the will: "In God I find supreme goodness, infinite wisdom, sweetness surpassing all understanding, superabundant charity, immense mercy, supreme clemency, and every perfection to the highest degree. I find that he is the one who created everything for your sake. He granted you your own noble being and he has preserved you until now. For your sake he became a man; for you he descended on earth; for you he suffered, fasted, wept;

for you he preached and laboured. He wandered only in search of you. Finally, for your sake, he let himself be seized, tied, scourged, and crucified. Now you may realize whether you should love him." And so the intellect describes all the benefits received by the will and God's infinite love for her.

Twenty-first, the will excites herself to draw intense acts of love from God.[16] She constrains and forces herself saying: "Lord, what can I give you in exchange for so many benefits? I have nothing except my love. I will willingly give it to you, though I am unworthy that you should accept it. Lord, I want only you as my bridegroom, friend, and father. You are my sole refuge, my only hope, my unique comfort. I want you to be my sole enjoyment, garden, rest, treasure, pleasure, delight, and all my glory. Oh sweet God, for your love I am happy to give up everything! With your love, I am happy to forsake all my friends in this world, my dear relatives, honours, vanities, pomp, wealth, and every delight. I am happy to deprive all my senses of the pleasures of this world, as far as I can. I am happy to risk my own life for your love. I would do it an infinite number of times, even if I were to resurrect infinite times. I choose to do it and I am happy to do it, though my senses and all my natural inclinations are against it. Even if I possessed an infinite number of worlds and were mistress of them all; even if, without ever dying, I could enjoy them forever with all possible pleasures and glory; yet, oh Lord, I would forsake them all for your love and I would rather be poor and serve you, the better to give you all my love. All the calumnies, infamies, dishonour, persecution, adversity, illnesses, penance, hardships, privations, poverty, and all the evils of the present life will never separate me from you. If it became necessary, for the sake of your love and honour, to step right into hell or even into infinite hells, I would do it right away in order to honour you. I would feel that I had done nothing in respect of what you deserve and of what I am bound to do. What can such a small creature as I am, do in exchange for your infinite love? I wish I could dissolve into nothingness. On the other hand, I wish I could possess a divine nature[17] to be able to give you infinite love. Even if I could be God, I wish I could go back to being nothing if that would increase your glory."

Twenty-second, she turns to the intellect and says: "From now on I will not have you indulge in wicked, filthy, or dishonest thoughts any more. Give up all useless, vain, fruitless thoughts; give up all speculative, idle knowledge! If I wish to be God's friend, I must be an enemy to all evil thoughts. Therefore, turn your back on everything! From now on I only want you to think of God. Let your eyes forever be fixed on him alone. Keep looking toward him and longing for him, so that you will inflame me all the more with divine love. Also, avoid inquiring into strange over-subtle things which are of no help to love but rather hinder it. Meditate with clear understanding and with all your power about God's perfection as an incitement to love. Make sure that you do not go wrong, for you would only be deceiving yourself."

Twenty-third, the intellect obeys, dwelling upon God with his thoughts for as long as possible.

Twenty-fourth, because of his constant dwelling on the thought of God, the will becomes pereniallly inflamed with divine love.

Twenty-fifth, the will perceives some resistance on the part of the senses. She orders the intellect to give careful consideration to all her natural inclinations, desires, and passions so as to curb them, restrain them and, as far as possible, turn them toward God. She says: "Check carefully where the fortress is closest to collapsing, in order to find a remedy. Keep an eye on all the doors of the senses, check on all that is required so that we may be safe from our enemies. I want no one but God to come into this fortress. It belongs to him and he is the only one who may inhabit it. I want it to be in perfect order."

Twenty-sixth, the intellect obeys. Surveying everything, he realizes that our sensitive powers and natural desires are like unbridled horses. They always run toward the honours, dignities, praise, and glory of this world; toward the wealth, pleasures, lust and possessions of this life. They are always in great danger of falling into the precipice of pride, greed, lust, and the other mortal sins. Therefore they stand in great need of the bridle of moderation. On the other hand, he sees that they behave like unwilling hacks in front of the steep hill of virtue. They refuse to gallop toward it. On the contrary, they try to avoid it and to go back. Clearly, they need a lot of spurring.

Twenty-seventh, the intellect informs the will of everything, saying: "Our desires are very unmanageable. A horse which is galloping toward a precipice should not be spurred. That is just what a man inclining to gluttony does when he tries hard to have delicious food. Such a horse should rather be reined in and fed less fodder. If he is unwilling to move, then he should be whipped and be kept alive only enough that he can go to God. One should never fail to spur him toward what is good. Oh will, we must place the greatest number of guards, take the greatest precautions, and concentrate our efforts where the fortress is weakest! We must offer the greatest resistance where we are most inclined."

Twenty-eighth, the will says: "You, intellect, can clearly perceive how necessary it is for everyone to know his own inclinations, desires, and passions, and also to know oneself well. No one can govern himself without that knowledge. Now I want you to tell me in greater detail how to rule my own feelings and all the kingdom of my soul."

Twenty-ninth, the intellect surveys everything: where the enemy may come in, where the fortress is weakest, the kind of watch that must be set up, all the weapons with which we must arm ourselves. In a word, all that is needed for our lives to be ordered in the best possible way.

Thirtieth, the intellect says to the will: "I find that the eyes are two very dangerous gates. One must take very good care of them and close them against all enemies. You must not open them to look at anything dishonest, strange or vain. If your eyes are forever fixed on the beauty of creation, you may easily fall in love with it. For that reason you must only open them to see what is necessary to human life and what promotes our love of God; for instance, the pious images of saints, of the Virgin Mary, and especially of Christ; also, holy inspiring books in which, as in clear mirrors and living images, you can see the virtues, deeds, examples, and lives of Christ, Mary, and God's chosen ones. You must contemplate Christ on the cross and his whole life. If any created beauty presents itself to you through your eyes, you must immediately command me, your intellect, not to dwell on that beauty. Thus you will not desire it and deprive God of the love which must be given to him alone. You must also do your best to prevent me from descending into some filthy evil thought following the promptings of some created beauty. I would drag you toward evil desires. If I am excited by vain, useless, fleeting beauty, let me rather reject it, soar high, and ascend in my thoughts to God's real beauty. Let me rest there and exhort you to love God. You must forbid your eyes to see and to choose all that is bad, dishonest, vain, strange, useless, and also futile. You must command them to open only to things which are necessary, useful, and leading to God's love."

Then, turning to your hearing, you will say: "From now on I do not want any infamy, slander or defamation, any dishonest or vengeful words, or any wicked words inciting to evil doing to come in through you. You will avoid them as well as all useless, strange or vain things. You will put aside all the stories, tales and news of the world, as well as all useless knowledge. You will reject all the words that hinder divine love or are of no use to it; you will avoid them and be deaf to them. You will only be open to God's words and you will strive to hear only those. I want you to have dealings only with people whose hearts dwell in God's love.[18] When they talk about Christ, their words are like flames which have the power to move me when they come in through you. If through you I hear some harmonious, sweet, delightful sound, some melodious voice or angelic song, then you, intellect, will neither dwell on it nor descend to some low thought.[19] Rather you will soar to the contemplation of the spiritual idea and harmony of the more than heavenly hierarchy of the three Divine Persons."

You will say to your smell: "I will not have any fragrant scents come in through you. They could come in as enemies and lead my senses toward evil. They could lure me into wicked desires and the intellect into wicked love, tainting my fancy and my other ladies-in-waiting and inner sensitive capacities. But if they come in as friends, prompting us and moving us to meditate about divine things and to love them, only then can they be let in."

You will also command your taste to feed frugally on whatever food is necessary to keep life all ordered in honour of God. It is enough for our vile bodies to eat enough to stay alive and to carry their burdens. But make sure that the body does not get so much food that it becomes unwilling to move. Take care that the mind is not confused by too many pleasures, so that the body ends up falling into some foul precipice.

"You, intellect, will rise to consider God's sweetness through the sweetness of earthly things. So you will incite me to love God. You, tongue, will no longer pronounce evil, useless, vain, or irrelevant words, but only words in honour of God, words which come from deep thought and meditation. Since you could easily ruin me, I want you to speak as few words as possible.

39

They must be useful, necessary, and full of wit; they must be born in and come from the depths of your heart and they must be rich in wisdom and all meant to honour God."

You must also command your feet not to move a single step unless it is to honour God. You must also control your hands so that they will do no evil, strange, vain, useless things, but only things which are necessary in a life devoted to God, the good of your fellow-beings, and the Lord's glory. "You, will, are our queen; you must control all our body so that its gestures, actions, motions, and operations may be slow, dignified, timely and orderly. You will also keep your ladies busy all the time. Let them conceive thoughts, exert their imagination, indulge their fancy, and busy themselves in God's service. If the reflection or image of something evil happens to insinuate itself among them, try to divert their attention at once and turn them toward the meditation of divine things." So the intellect tells the will all that she must do to introduce perfect order into human life.

Thirty-first, the will imparts commands to all her faculties and carries out all the suggestions of the intellect. She plans her life every day as if it were the last one.

Thirty-second, the intellect tells the will that in order to be more certain she must avoid all opportunities to do evil and she must seek opportunities to do good.

Thirty-third, the will commands the intellect to reveal such opportunities to her after he has tried to know them well.

Thirty-fourth, the intellect carries out the will's orders, reviewing all his external enemies and their snares. He also reviews his friends and the way in which their help may be obtained.

Thirty-fifth, he says to the will: "You have many enemies, but they cannot do you any harm so long as you are your own friend. You hold the keys of the fortress; no one can come in without your consent.

You will not be defeated unless you want to be. You must avoid evil company and consort only with good people from whom you may acquire some virtue. If you associate with someone and notice that you have developed too sensual an attachment to him, leave him alone. Do not have so much to do with him and let all your love end in God. If there is someone whom you do not like, do not let that stop you from being good to him. Try to overcome your own feelings and the reluctance of your senses. If you enjoy honours, try always to humble yourself; if you enjoy wealth, give many alms; if you are fond of pleasure, mortify your body with continuous penance. Stay as far away as possible from the love of the world; have nothing to do with it, all the more since it is all corrupt. If you cannot help living with people and associating with them, do not let your love dwell on them. At least let your love spring up to God.[20] Be high-minded; let all the things of this world look like nothing to you; learn to despise them."

Thirty-sixth, the will begins to carry out his orders and to lead a virtuous life.

Thirty-seventh, the intellect says: "Never look back. Follow the path of love and never give up till you reach the end. Do not let yourself be detained by worldly honour, false pleasure or vain wealth, by friends or family, by the crowd or by bad examples. Let Christ be part of you and let him be your guide."

Thirty-eighth, the intellect says: "Let your love grow greater every day and never think yourself perfect. If you ever happened to think that you have reached your goal, you would really be coming to a halt. If you stopped walking forward you would necessarily move back."

Thirty-ninth, the intellect says: "Be of a willing disposition and do not worry if you do not reach your goal too soon."

Fortieth, "Walk with even steps; do not let your true love of God decline either in prosperity or in adversity.

If you are lukewarm you will always waver at the thought of the earthly things you are forsaking. Look toward God alone with fervour."

Forty-first, the intellect says: "Always be on your guard while you are in this life, even if you happened to be more saintly than the saints themselves. Do not rely on yourself; live in fear and place all your hope in God."

Forty-second, "Always obey divine inspiration and the admonitions of the Holy Spirit."

Forty-third, "Make sure that you often place yourself in God's hands with all your heart."

Forty-fourth, "Whatever you do, you can never feel that your actions are good enough. You must attribute all that is good to God, and ascribe all the glory to him and all sins to yourself. They would be infinitely more numerous if God did not constantly help you with his grace."

Forty-fifth, "Do not be ungrateful. Attribute all that is good in yourself to God and give him all praise, honour and glory."

Forty-sixth, "With your life, good examples, words, prayers, and in every possible way try to attract toward God all those who are capable of receiving him."

Forty-seventh, "Throughout all your life give no thought to yourself or to your own comfort, profit, honour or pleasure. Do not follow devious intents. Rather, let your intentions be simple and straightforward, meant only to please God and to give him honour and glory."

Forty-eighth, "Let all your hope and trust be placed in God. Expect all good only from him."

Forty-ninth, the will now leads a virtuous life by divine grace and also because of her acquired good habits. The way to God, which at first seemed steep to her, now begins to appear easy.

Fiftieth, the intellect applauds and praises her because she has obeyed him and lives according to God's will. So she begins to enjoy heaven in the present life.

The end.

IV

A DIALOGUE ABOUT
THE THIEF ON THE CROSS

Characters: a Man and a Woman

WOMAN: Who is not overwhelmed on seeing the abyss of divine judgment? Christ was on the cross; his flesh was all lacerated; he was close to dying; he had been denied by Peter, betrayed by Judas, abandoned by the others, persecuted by the Jews and mocked by the Gentiles. No one believed in him except his sorrowful mother, the glorious Virgin Mary. And now a poor thief began to have faith in him, when all the others failed. Yet they had spoken with Christ, they had heard his evangelical teachings. They had seen his innocent life, his supreme virtues, his overabundant charity, his extreme, holy, profound humility, his wonderful deeds, signs, and miracles. They had read the prophets, they had studied the Scriptures and their symbols[1] and they had seen them all come true in Christ. In spite of that they did not believe in him. Not only was he hanging from the cross, unable to perform miracles; he also did not appear in the least glorious in his divine deeds. Just then a poor thief, with no understanding or knowledge, who had not read or seen the Scriptures and who knew nothing about signs or miracles, a thief who had never even seen or heard Christ before, who was himself on the cross in anguish and pain, believed that Christ was God, seeing him in such agony and so close to death. He trusted that he would obtain heaven from one who was hanging on the cross and crying: "My God, my God, why have you deserted me?".[2] I would like you to tell me what inspired him with such a strong faith.

43

MAN: Some said that Christ's shadow fell upon him and that the thief was illuminated by it; just as St. Peter's shadow cured the sick.[3] So Christ illuminated the thief. For not only has Christ, the light of this world, abundantly illuminated us with his teaching and life. So also has Christ's shadow, that is, the Old Testament, which is like the shadow of the New one and is enough to give us the necessary understanding of Christ's divinity. Others said that Mary was standing on the side of the thief, that she was looking at Christ and that Christ was looking at her, so their visual rays brushed past the thief and he was illuminated.

WOMAN: Please tell me what you think about it.

MAN: Looking at Christ, the good thief saw that he was not perturbed by his own suffering. On the contrary, his face looked happy, as if he were actually rejoicing in the shedding of his own blood. The thief could see Christ's burning tears falling on the ground and Christ's ardent fervent sighs going up to heaven. He could hear Christ's loving words; he could contemplate Christ's divine gestures and actions, his admirable patience, his abundant charity, his long endurance and his other divine virtues. Seeing all that, the thief could not help believing that Christ was indeed the Son of God.

God never fails those who are disposed to receive him. The thief was as disposed as his own frailty allowed, so Christ illuminated him. If the other thief had also been disposed to the best of his ability, then with the help of unfailing divine grace, Christ would have illuminated him too. Just as Christ, who alone is true and divine,[4] was born and lived for the sake of us all, so he also died for all men. Christ looked at the good thief with the eyes of his mercy,[5] and perhaps also with his corporeal eyes, as he had looked at Peter. The thief was also a symbol of the elect who will be at Christ's right. They will go to heaven not through our merits, but through the merits of Christ;[6] the wicked at his left will be damned for their evil deeds.

The thief was also saved so that no one should despair, seeing that such a wicked thief had reached salvation at the last moment. He had mocked Christ even after he was nailed to the cross, as one reads in Matthew XXVII.[7] Therefore he was an image of all the elect who are saved only by the goodness, kindness and mercy of God.

It was natural that a thief should be illuminated and saved on Good Friday, when the doors opened to disclose all the divine treasures[8] and when Christ shed his blood with such fervour; the new wine of divine love bursting forth from his wounds and grace raining upon earth in such abundance.[9] Oh how great were the thief's faith, hope, and love! He offered Christ his heart and all his love; his thoughts, tongue and words. Above all, he offered himself on the cross, first by confessing not only his own sins, but also those of all sinners, whose symbol he was. As may be read in Luke, XXIII, he said: "We are rightly punished; we are receiving what we deserve for our evil deeds and we must bear it patiently."[10] The wicked do the opposite. They think that they are in the right and, like the unrepentant thief, they say: "If you are Christ," as if they doubted it, "then save yourself and us." They refuse to be punished as they deserve, almost as if they were saying: "What need is there for me to pray to your Father? If you are Christ, then save yourself and us," as if they really meant, "You are not Christ, so you cannot save yourself." The bad grow worse the more they suffer, but the good open their eyes when they are punished and they acknowledge Christ, just as the good thief did when he was on the cross.

By confessing his own sins he acknowledged that he was being rightly punished. He defended Christ's innocence saying: "This man has not sinned; he is suffering for us and for our faults because of his pure goodness and excessive charity. We must pity him and thank him, since he is suffering for us, not for himself, so that by his prayers we may be forgiven." He also rebuked the bad thief saying: "You have no fear of God, though you are on the cross and near death." Then he prayed with these words: "My Lord Christ, remember me when you come into your kingdom."[11] Notice how he acknowledged Christ's divinity by calling him Lord! Notice how full of divine wisdom faith is! He did not beg for something transitory, but for something divine — only that Christ should remember him.[12] Notice his profound humility, almost as if he meant to say: "I do not deserve to be in heaven near you with the other saints or to live in paradise with the blessed spirits. Let me at least live in your memory. Even if I am damned, it will be enough for me that you will remember me from time to time. If I know that you will remember me, then I will consider myself happy even if I am in eternal torment."

Oh what great fortitude and steadfastness! Being on the cross in such torment, he rose above himself and only thought of Christ. He placed himself in God's hands with supreme humbleness, meting out everything with the greatest fairness: glory and honour to God, torment and punishment to himself, and rebuke to the bad thief. That is why Christ answered him so kindly: "In truth I say, this day you shall be with me in heaven."[13] Not only did Christ promise him heaven, but to make the promise more certain he added: "In truth," almost as if to say: "Be certain, do not doubt, even if you have been a wicked thief, and even if you see me suffering on the cross. In spite of all, today we shall be in heaven together." Notice what a great gift Christ gave him when the thief had only asked to be remembered! Christ promised him paradise. When? That very day. With whom? With Christ. Oh, in what company! And for how long? Forever. To whom did Christ make such a promise? To a worthless thief who was on the cross for his crimes and who had insulted him only a short time before.[14] Why did Christ promise him paradise? Only because the thief had begged to be remembered.

WOMAN: I feel certain that he is in heaven, since Christ said so. I also believe that he is a great saint and that he enjoys many special favours.[15]

MAN: First of all, he alone among all the elect deserved to suffer the torment of the cross together with Christ and to be in his company. He alone shared in his heart the holy Virgin's faith in Christ and her sorrow for him. On that day, when everyone else abandoned Christ, he alone fearlessly and publicly proclaimed Christ's innocence and divinity from his pulpit, which was the cross. He rebuked the other thief and perhaps also the other Jews. I think he also addressed words of comfort to the Virgin Mary, though the evangelists did not record them.[16] When the Virgin Mary heard that he was to be in heaven with Christ that day, imagine how willingly she must have adopted him as her own son together with her St. John. How much happier than all the rest of the elect she must have considered him to be!

The thief begged for grace when Christ was pouring it out on everyone and when, by dying for all, he was bestowing it on all. It is to be believed that the thief received an abundant share of it, the more so since the fortress of Christ's wound was open on the side where the thief was.[17] Therefore he was an image of all the elect. I think that he stands by Christ's side in his glory just as he was by Christ's side on the cross. When a king is slandered and accused by everyone, nothing can please him better than for at least one man to excuse him, defend him, and bear witness to his innocence and goodness, just as the thief did for Christ. When we are troubled, we can learn from him to say: "We are suffering with good reason, according to what we deserve; only Christ suffered unjustly."

Therefore, the thief meant to say: "I have read about Abel and Cain; that they were brothers and that one of them pleased God, while the other one did not. Instead, he fell into despair."[18] Though he was on the cross, like the other thief, he refused to give in to

47

despair saying: "Perhaps he will forgive me. I have also read about Noah, who was mocked by his own son, Cam, and covered in his nakedness by Sem. For that reason one was cursed, while the other one was blessed.[19] It is my duty to defend you and perhaps you will bless me. Also Abraham had two children, one by a free woman, the other one by a slave.[20] My companion wishes to be the son of the synagogue and to be inspired by fear and servitude. That is why he is so restless. Instead, I wish to try and be the first child of the holy church, your new bride, and to be inspired by love, as all good children are. Isaac had two sons, Jacob and Esau; one of them did not care at all for his own inheritance, while the other one tried to obtain it.[21] Even if my companion does not care for heaven, yet I will strive to reach it."

So the thief meant to say: "When you are in your own kingdom, whose natural heir you are and which you purchased for us with your own precious blood; when you are not great in this world, for your kingdom is not of this world, but in your own heavenly kingdom; then remember me, not the sins, errors, worthlessness, and robberies of which I am guilty. Remember that I am a frail miserable man, that I was created by you in your likeness and image, and that you made me capable of achieving heavenly happiness. Remember that you created everything for me, that for me you became man, for me you preached, fasted, prayed, slept on the ground, laboured, and suffered for thirty-three years. Remember that I am related to you and that you are dying for me. I am not asking for great things, because I do not deserve them. I am ashamed to beg that you should allow such a great scoundrel as me to go to heaven. I know that is not the place for me, I know that you have a thousand reasons not to want me there. I am not asking to be allowed to go to paradise and to serve heaven's citizens. I certainly do not deserve that. I am only asking to be in your memory. You must not forget those for whom you are shedding so much blood and suffering so much, your fellow-sufferers on the cross. Do not consider my malice but your own perfect goodness which has opened the doors to reveal your treasures. I am begging for alms, hoping to obtain grace. If it were possible, I would like to steal heaven in my last hour, just as I stole the things of this world when I was alive. I have heard you pray to your Father for those who have nailed you on the cross, gently forgiving them saying that they do not know what they are doing. Therefore do not be surprised if I dare to pray to you. I have seen that you have entrusted your mother to be mother to all sinners, so that with burning love she should thirst for our salvation. That is why I have dared to pray to you. I am on the cross, as you can see, and I have three crosses in my heart which are far bitterer than this one: one is the sorrow I feel for my companion, who has not repented; another one is my fear of hell; the third one is the compassion I feel for you and your mother. Even so, if I only knew that you will remember me when you are in heaven, all my crosses would be sweet to me."

Then Christ replied: "Today is the day of eternity when nothing is, was, or will be — all is now. You shall be (for we are still immersed in time) with me in heaven, because you shall see my divine essence. You shall see me drawing with me from Limbo all the saintly spirits in the Old Testament;[22] you shall see the heavens open up and then you shall ascend to the Empyrean[23] with the other blessed spirits. There you shall forever enjoy my vision in triumph and glory."

In his absence, Christ wants us to address gentle words to the sick and to the dying. He began to give their daily wages to the very last hired, as is said in St. Matthew, XX beginning with the thief.[24] He said to the first thief: "You are dust and you shall return to dust." To the last one in the Old Testament he said: "Today you shall be in heaven with me."[25] The thief is really in heaven. I know that he is on the cross for

Christ, suffering on the point of death only for his love.

Just like Christ, we too shall be on the cross when we go through the agonies of death; we shall be in the middle of two thieves, the good angel and the bad one, and often also in the middle of relatives who will be standing around us like real thieves waiting to grab our possessions, taking no care of our souls. Therefore it is better to give our things away and to get ready now, for it is hard to prepare oneself when one has to die. The thief's conversion was not only Christ's last miracle; it was also his greatest. Therefore Your Grace[26] should not delay or despair, if you should ever find yourself in such a situation. Like the good thief you must try to live forever, but not in the memory of the people of this world. That would be of no use to you and you would soon be forgotten. Instead, you must seek to live happily in Christ's memory through love and virtue. Christ in his glory will certainly not forget us if we always remember the bitter suffering of his Passion.

The end.

V

A DIALOGUE ABOUT THE NEED TO BE CONVERTED EARLY

Characters: Christ and a Soul

CHRIST: How can you be so uncourteous? I am the Son of God, I am supreme beauty. I have long been calling you to heaven, day after day, not for my own but for your sake. Yet you are deaf, unkind, and ungrateful. You refuse to answer, but you are kind and grateful to the things of this world. You never fail to do your duty to them. I am the only one to whom you pay no attention at all.

SOUL: I may be slow in coming to you, yet I am full of good will.

CHRIST: If you were full of good will, you would prove it.

SOUL: One must give such things a great deal of thought. Such steps may be taken only once, so one must give them serious consideration.

CHRIST: It is certainly advisable to consider doubtful matters carefully. Also, when one intends to do something bad one should give it a lot of serious thinking. But everyone should be resolute and ready to serve God.

SOUL: For the moment I cannot leave this worthless world without losing face. There are many who would say that I am being rejected by it, so I want to wait until things begin to get better for me and the world smiles at me again.[1] Then I will trample it underfoot and show everyone that I can see through it and that I am giving it up, not because of fear or anger, but for the sake of your love.

CHRIST: What if the world never smiles at you?

SOUL: I would just leave it anyway.

CHRIST: Those who depend on people's opinions cannot be happy. One who is bound by so many considerations cannot ascend to God. Wanting to come to me without losing your worldly honour is like wanting to serve two enemies. Whoever truly wants to come to me must not only give up his honour and everything else: he must give himself up. So, the thought of your worldly honour is stronger in holding you back than my love is in making you leave everything! If your love for me were perfect, the world with all its chains would not be able to delay you by even the twinkling of an eye. This is not the way I behaved toward you! On the contrary, for your sake I despised everything and I was held in contempt. Enough of this shilly-shallying! Make a bundle of all the good and evil spoken by the world! Throw it behind you, treat it with the contempt which it deserves or else you will never achieve any good!

Let us pretend that the world were to hold you in great esteem.[2] Perhaps it would bind you with its enticements much more tightly than you are bound now. How great it feels to presume to say: "I will not be enticed by the delights of this world, I will win where Lucifer, Adam, David, Solomon, and some other great soldiers of God lost!" People change as the world changes. Whoever does not seize God's favours when he has them does not deserve a second chance. Time is precious. You should not waste it like this, especially considering that the future is so uncertain.

SOUL: If I give up the world now, everyone will have something to say about it. I would rather not be criticized by the world. Once a wise man was heard to curse those who neglect to protect their own reputation.

CHRIST: That only applies to sinners, who are infamous in the eyes of the world. Honour and all other things may only be loved to the extent to which they are a help in rising to God. If they are a hindrance or if they are useless, then they must be given up and forgotten.

SOUL: I would rather not leave the world in such a rush.

CHRIST: I see: you would like to have your cake and eat it too.[3] You would like to serve me without being an enemy to the world, which is impossible.

SOUL: I have come to care very little for its caresses. It is true, though, that I would not like it to criticize me; so, I am trying to detach myself from it a little at a time.

CHRIST: That is a sure sign that your love for me is not strong enough. If you really loved me, you would certainly not mind having the world as your enemy. On the contrary, you would be proud of it. Have you forgotten the torments and insults the world dealt me for thirty-three years? Yet, in order to save you and to expose its deceits I associated with it. You have forgotten the shame, the false calumnies, the scourgings, the thorns, and the cross the world gave me. It was always an enemy to me and to my friends. Yet you are trying to please it, or at least you would rather not displease it. A fine way for you to avenge your bridegroom! This is the faith you pledged to me at your baptism; these are your promises, gratitude, and mutual love; this is the reward for my labours; this is the way in which you follow me bearing your cross!

Let us suppose for a moment that you will pay no attention to me or to my honour. Let us suppose that you have completely forgotten the insults the world has hurled at me and the saints. Let us suppose that you have forgotten how it has always persecuted us, being an enemy to all virtue. In any case, it would be in your own interest to hate it and detest it for all it has done to you. If you would just open your eyes, you would realize that it has always done the worst possible things to you. Is it not true that it has played many dirty tricks on you and all its smiles and chuckles have been false and only meant to deceive you better? Is it not true that so far it has never stopped doing you as much harm as it could, so that sometimes it has required miracles on my part to free you from it?

In spite of that you are still trying to ingratiate it, whereas, if you had a gentle heart, its mere sight should be enough to make you furious.

I let it kick you when you thought that it was being nice to you, only to help you to realize what a traitor it really is. Considering your obstinacy and seeing that you refuse to budge even though I pull you toward me, I have ordered the world to reject you. You will have to give it up by force, since you will not do so by love. Just go on: do not displease the world, stay friends with it, hold it in great respect, make sure that you do not incur its criticism, be kind to it, smile at it, do not give it up so soon, put it off a little longer! Perhaps death will come in the meantime. You certainly have no such consideration for me. You do not care whether you displease me or insult me. On the contrary, the more I do for you, the less I get in return.

SOUL: I have been gradually detaching myself from the world for many days. I will soon come to you.

CHRIST: Those who think that they can untie, one at a time, all the little chains by which men are tied to the world, think that they can achieve the impossible. That is one of the world's favourite tricks. As soon as one chain is untied, seven others become tied up, because one matter relates to twenty-five others. One must make a clean cut and detach oneself from the world once and for all. It is like birdlime: when you are trying to clean yourself up, the more you handle it the stickier your hands get. The world is just like an impetuous, violent, rapid stream. Those who expect to cross it a little at a time, walking slowly, and taking frequent rests, often deceive themselves and end up engulfed by the current. We must run the whole course of our lives vigorously, energetically, and strongly, without ever stopping to catch our breath.

SOUL: After so many hardships I had hoped to reach the harbour and to be at peace.

CHRIST: Your ship is built in such a way that she can reach the harbour with any wind, so long as you wish to do so. In fact, she can reach the harbour much better when the wind blows against her than when it fills her sails. If, in order to be at peace, you wait for the world itself to be at peace, to go the way you want it to go, and to be in perfect order, you are greatly deceived. That will never happen. Your desires are too insatiable; the things of this world are so inextricably confused that they will never come to an end. So you must not wait for the sea to lie still and for motion to come to an end. You must rather set yourself and your desires at peace, and then you will find yourself in the harbour. Cast the anchor of your hope[4] in me and you will be still. Otherwise you will strive in vain.

SOUL: I may delay, but in any case I will come to you in the end.

CHRIST: Why do you delay? Why are you uncertain? Why do you hesitate to come to me? Perhaps you will run out of time. Then you will regret the time you wasted, but in vain. God is too high a prize. A wise man must always be sure of himself and must not keep saying: "I will do well," without ever making a start. Nearly all those who are now in hell; once thought that they would change their lives, yet they failed. Make sure that does not happen to you too.

SOUL: Come on! Let us begin!

CHRIST: You are not so fast as I wish. If you delay you are lost.

SOUL: Would you expect me to leave all my affairs in a state of confusion?

CHRIST: Would you expect to disentangle the tangled maze of this inextricable world, which has always been and will always be an utter chaos of confusion?

SOUL: I have had only one relief in all my troubles and anguish.

CHRIST: What was that?

SOUL: A firm hope that I should be free one day. Otherwise I would have fallen into despair.

CHRIST: It is usual for those who feel miserable to indulge in and feed on hopes which often turn out to be vain. I would not like that to happen to you. Your day of freedom will never come. If you follow your senses, you will never find the time or the way to come to me. You can see for yourself that the world is rejecting you. It does not smile on you, even though you are happy. On the contrary, it looks harsh and threatening. Imagine what it could do to you if it saw you in a state of utter despair! On the other hand, I never fail to call you in every possible way, at all times. Have I not enabled you to understand me and my great sincere love? I know that you often enjoy the perception of my sweetness, though you are unworthy of it. Why do you delay? All the obstacles are removed, all the impediments are eliminated, all the chains are broken. The world will never be without many who will take care of it. The day which you so eagerly awaited, when you are to be set free, has come at last! What are you doing then, why do you linger, whom are you waiting for? Do you perhaps imagine that I will remove you from this worthless world by force? I do not need you. Your coming does not increase my glory, nor does your delay cause me any sorrow.

SOUL: As you know, I had already intended to leap up[5] and come to you when I was tied with far more chains than now. Imagine what I shall do now that I am set free!

CHRIST: How many times you will feel sorry that it has taken you so long!

SOUL: In St. Matthew, XXII, you say that first one has to render unto Caesar what is Caesar's and then unto God what is God's.[6] Therefore we must first satisfy the world and render unto it what belongs to it.

CHRIST: That is to say pomp, pride, vanity, ignorance, ingratitude, deceit, falsehood, betrayal, delights, concupiscence, greed, and all its other vices and miseries. That is what you must render unto it, so that you may become immaculately pure and give God praise, honour, and glory.

SOUL: I think that I may save some fellow-being by delaying.

CHRIST: Save yourself first! To be in danger and to attempt to save your friends is like seeking your own death and that of others, too. First tie yourself inseparably to me. Can you not see that the boat leaks and that everyone is trying to save his own life? This is not the time to think about your things or your friends. Let each one fend for himself.

SOUL: I wish to fulfil my obligations first.

CHRIST: It will please me to see you free yourself from all your past or future obligations. It is better that you should give away most of what you have, than that you should remain in debt by one penny. One must make absolutely sure, paying no attention to personal honour or to property when God's honour is at stake. Unless a patient has taken a strong laxative, nothing that he eats will sit well with him. On the contrary, everything will be bad for him. The same would happen to you. Therefore you must make sure that you empty the stomach of your own conscience really well before you come to me. Hurry up! Do not wait until your head is on the block![7] Give up your sins, or better, make them give you up! The longer you wait, the farther away from me you will go and the harder it will be for you to come back. Your bad habits will grow stronger and stronger. Why wait then? Consider my love. Do not render vain all my labours; do not render fruitless the shedding of my blood. Feel compassion for me, if not for yourself. You know very well that you no longer belong to yourself, and that I gave up my life for you. I am waiting for you with my arms on the Cross. I am inviting you, calling you to heaven. If you will come to me, I will truly forgive you everything. You will be my cherished, well-beloved, dear bride, and you will triumph with me forever.

The end

VI

DIALOGUE ABOUT THE PILGRIMAGE TO HEAVEN

Characters: a Guardian Angel and a Pilgrim Soul

PILGRIM SOUL: *(aside)* I am a pilgrim in this world. I know that this is not my fatherland, so I can find no rest.[1] I have only one day to spend here and heaven, on the other side, is eternal. Where shall I go, unhappy me? How blind I was to lovingly dwell on the things of the world! I have tried to make a home out of a place of exile; I have tried to stand firm on water. The world has always rejected me, giving me nothing but anguish and showing me all its miseries and calamities. In spite of that, I have not yet stopped loving it. On the contrary, I have clung to it more and more. God often illuminated me and showed me that heaven was my real home. He called me, but I played deaf and did not answer him. All that I cared for was to amass riches, to build palaces, to make gardens, to acquire possessions, to seek honours and dignities, and to be loved by the people of this world as if I were to be here forever.

In a word, I have been so blind that I have tried to make a perpetual heaven out of this worthless world, which is a real hell, in which I have to spend only a few days. Oh, miserable me! I have not yet come any closer to God and to my real home during all the time in which I have lived in the world. Or rather during all the time in which I have failed to live; for, from day to day I have become more and more estranged from real life. The time has come for me to open my eyes and to realize my own fatal mistake. I will change

59

my ways, leave this despicable world, say good-bye to all my friends, and begin my journey to heaven. But since I might easily go wrong and miss the way, I would need a good guide. I could not think of a better one than the angel who always guards me and keeps me company. I want to have a talk with him.

(to the angel) Tell me, dear brother and companion on the way to God, what do I require in order to reach my fatherland?

GUARDIAN ANGEL: The three Divine Persons were never pilgrims. They were always in their own homeland, always in heaven in supreme glory and happiness. They never walked along the path of merit, they never progressed from one virtue to the next one. On the contrary, they were perfect to the highest degree from eternity. Their love of the Godhead was infinite; they could not come any closer to God with greater love. Therefore they could not walk to God as pilgrims along the path of love.

We angels were pilgrims once. We were created and placed outside heaven, so that we had to approach God by the path of love. The wicked angels walked along the path of self-love and reached the city of Babylon; the good ones followed the path of divine love and came into the heavenly Jerusalem, the lofty City of Heaven.[2]

Your early parents in Earthly Paradise were pilgrims too, but because of the sin of disobedience they were driven away, confined in this world, and even declared rebels. The gates of heaven were closed so that no one could enter before Christ. Though many saintly spirits knocked on the door of divine mercy, yet it did not open. They went to Limbo, though they were saintly.

To the extent that he was human, Christ was partly a pilgrim, but partly he was not. He enjoyed the vision of God[3] and he was a pilgrim in his own fatherland. On his way he gathered merit, not for himself but for us. He was always in his heavenly homeland with the higher part of his soul, but he was on his way to heaven with the lower part. By his great suffering he caused the gates of heaven to open and he made it possible for you to be blessed again. That is why you are no longer rebels. You are reconciled by Christ's most precious blood. You are all pilgrims and you can be saved. Since God has entrusted me with taking special care of you, I will illuminate you and give you every possible help to lead you to God.

PILGRIM SOUL: If I wish to go to heaven, my fatherland, I think that I will have to give up the world and turn my back on it. I would like to know what to do in order to depart.

GUARDIAN ANGEL: Before leaving the world you must settle all your debts. If you have something that belongs to your neighbour, return it; if you have wrecked someone's honour or reputation, take back your words; if you have taken someone's life or done damage or harm to his body, offer the best compensation you can; if you have sown the tares of discord among people and destroyed the good holy love and peace that reigned among them before, you must offer some satisfaction and try to bring people back to their previous condition; if in any way you have induced a fellow-being to sin with your words, life, or example, depriving him of God, heaven, and divine grace, you must first give him back all those things in whichever way you can; in a word, you must pay off all your debts once and for all. If you must fulfil the terms of a will, see that you carry out all your obligations; if you have made any vows or promises, fulfil them. As long as you are tied, if you neglect to untie yourself and to do your duty, you will never be able to ascend to God.

PILGRIM SOUL: What if I cannot carry out all those obligations?

GUARDIAN ANGEL: Do the best you can. If you lack power, use your good will. Do you know what you should do?

PILGRIM SOUL: What?

GUARDIAN ANGEL: You should make a public announcement, informing everyone that you wish to leave and that, if anyone feels that you owe him something, he should let you know and you will pay him. So if you happen to have a debt which you do not know about or which you cannot remember, you will be able to pay it.

PILGRIM SOUL: I would feel ashamed to make such an announcement.

GUARDIAN ANGEL: On the contrary, it would be a generous noble action. When the rich lords of this world have spent some time visiting a place and they decide to leave, they send announcements saying that anyone to whom they owe money should claim it within a certain period of time and he will get paid, because they are leaving. You have all the more reason to do that since you have been in this world for such a long time and you have a longer way to go. If you fail to pay off your debts through your own carelessness, you will not be able to move or to take even one step on the way to God. Therefore you must cancel all such obligations to the world. Whoever is bound by them cannot ascend to God.

PILGRIM SOUL: What else must I do?

GUARDIAN ANGEL: Sell all your possessions, palaces and movable property.

PILGRIM SOUL: That is asking too much.

GUARDIAN ANGEL: What good are they to you? In any case, you are leaving. Indeed, as Christ said in St. Matthew, XIX, you must sell everything.[4] Anything that you leave behind will be lost. You must send your carriages ahead of you, if you expect to be rich when you get to heaven. As Christ said in St. Matthew, VI: "Store up your treasures in heaven."[5]

PILGRIM SOUL: To whom shall I give my things that they may be safely taken to heaven?

GUARDIAN ANGEL: To Christ and his poor.

PILGRIM SOUL: What if I myself take them along?

GUARDIAN ANGEL: You would not be able to walk carrying such weight. One must be light and fast in order to walk such a long distance. There could also be highwaymen who might rob you or kill you on the way, and so you would lose everything.

PILGRIM SOUL: May I not keep anything?

GUARDIAN ANGEL: Only whatever you require for your daily needs and no more.

PILGRIM SOUL: I have many children, relatives and friends. Must I leave everyone behind?

GUARDIAN ANGEL: I certainly do not want you to leave anyone behind. On the contrary, you must try to take them all along with you in a happy group.

PILGRIM SOUL: What if they refuse to come?

GUARDIAN ANGEL: Then just leave them alone and go by yourself, even if your own father refused to come. Do you not know that in St. Matthew, X, Christ said that those who love their fathers or mothers more than they love him do not deserve him?[6]

PILGRIM SOUL: So you expect me to go alone.

GUARDIAN ANGEL: It is better to be saved alone than to be damned in company.

PILGRIM SOUL: I have a sister who is the apple of my eye. What if she refuses to come?

GUARDIAN ANGEL: Just turn your back on her. Do you not know what Christ said in St. Matthew, V? "It is better to go to heaven with only one eye than to hell with two."[7] So, even if your sister is the apple of your eye, pluck the eye out of your head, remove her from your heart, and turn to God.

PILGRIM SOUL: I have a brother who does everything for me. He manages my household and I could not possibly live without him. It would be like having my hands cut off.

GUARDIAN ANGEL: If he will not come or, even worse, if he proves to be an obstacle on your way to God, cut him away from you according to what Christ says in St. Matthew, V: "Even if he were your right hand."[8]

PILGRIM SOUL: What must I do in order to induce them to come with me?

GUARDIAN ANGEL: You must enlighten them, persuade them to follow Christ, help them, rebuke them, correct them, and do as much good to them as you can with your words, examples, life, and prayers.

PILGRIM SOUL: I occupy a high position in life.

GUARDIAN ANGEL: Give it up if it prevents you from following this path.

PILGRIM SOUL: What about the pleasures I used to enjoy in this world?

GUARDIAN ANGEL: You must give up everything for love and take your leave of all creatures. You must not wait until you die, for then you will have to give things up by force and that will not please God.

PILGRIM SOUL: Tell me how to go to God.

GUARDIAN ANGEL: That is done through love. The more you love God, the faster you go. If you love creation more than you love God, then you move one step forward and two back again; you will never get there. If you loved God as much as you love creation, you would never make any progress. So if you wish to be closer to God every day, you must love God more than you love yourself and every other creature. If you love creation but you also love God much more, then you will move two steps forward and one back. You will still make some progress, though you will be somewhat slowed down by creation. But if you loved God alone you would find no obstacles on your way. The more intensely you loved him, the faster you would go to God.

PILGRIM SOUL: When must I begin?

GUARDIAN ANGEL: In the early morning if you wish your day to be fruitful. Begin in your youth, for it is then that one walks most vigorously.

PILGRIM SOUL: But I am already old.

GUARDIAN ANGEL: At least do not put it off any longer.

PILGRIM SOUL: I should hate to miss the way.

GUARDIAN ANGEL: Keep walking straight on. Do not turn right or left because of prosperity or adversity. Let your intention always be well aimed and keep your eyes riveted on God. If God's honour is the purpose of your walking, you cannot fail. The honours, riches, and pleasures of this life, as well as your friends and relatives will come forward to meet you. They will try to stop you with their enticements, saying: "Where are you leaving us? Why are you going away? Why are you not staying with us?" They will try to hold you back. You must be prudent and careful. You must shut your eyes and turn your back on them, so that your love of them will not stop you. Follow the example of other pilgrims. When they walk past some beautiful city, they just cast a glance without even stopping. That is what you must do in this world.

PILGRIM SOUL: I think I will find it very hard to walk such a long way.

GUARDIAN ANGEL: The first step, which will carry you over the threshold, that is, making up your mind, is the hardest one. But when one is truly disposed to change one's life; when one begins to walk along the path to God, nothing is too hard as one gets farther and farther away from the world and closer to God. Love bears every burden easily and endures every hardship without difficulty. If the road seems too hard to you sometimes, just pretend that you are a man returning home: when the road is hard he remembers that he will soon see his father, mother, brothers, relatives, and friends again and he imagines their warm welcome. So he does not even realize that he is still walking. That is what you must do. Think of Christ, the Virgin Mary, and all the saints; imagine the glory and rejoicing in heaven when you will arrive there. Keep on walking with joy, singing with a blissful feeling in your heart and mind as you go!

Try to have some companion on your way with whom to talk about God. There are some who give no thought to the road. If you happen to need a rest, take shelter in the wound on Christ's side.[9] You will regain your strength and your fervour will immediately increase. Beware of backsliding, as happened to God's chosen people when they decided to return to Egypt. Rather you must walk forward every day and become better and better on your way to God. To stop and not to wish to improve is tantamount to growing worse and sliding back.

65

PILGRIM SOUL: Tell me what clothes to wear.

GUARDIAN ANGEL: You should be poorly dressed in coarse clothes so that your bare needs may be satisfied. Learn from the pilgrims of this world. Though they may be great lords at home, yet they go on pilgrimages incognito and poorly dressed so as to avoid being taken prisoners somewhere. You must do the same. Hide the treasures, gifts, and spiritual riches the eternal God may have given you, so that vainglory will not take them away from you.

PILGRIM SOUL: Could I not show them off in order to increase God's glory?

GUARDIAN ANGEL: Then you should not hide them, but you should show them as something belonging to him.

PILGRIM SOUL: What if someone affronts me on the way?

GUARDIAN ANGEL: Do not stop or go back to seek your revenge. Walking toward God must be your only aim; you must disregard everything else. A pilgrim does not stop to argue, he does not go asking for trouble.[10] He does not intrigue or pay any attention to what goes on in the world. He does not try to acquire honours, friends or riches while he is on his way, because his intent is to walk on. He cannot find any city so beautiful that it does not look ugly to him by comparison with his own city. The customs of the citizens of this world appear clumsy to him by comparison with those of heaven. He cannot be satisfied by any wealth, treasures, honours, dignities, pleasures, friends, relatives or anything else in this life. He continually sighs for his fatherland. Like Paul, he wishes to die and be with Christ[11] and he says: "When will the day come when I shall die at last and go to heaven?"

So long as he is in the present life, he feels as if he were in a dirty stable. He does not hold the world to be worth a bean.[12] He is here only because he cannot help it. He cannot sleep very much because of his intense desire to go on. He only eats what is enough to enable him to stay alive and go to God. He is careful not to overburden himself with too much food, because that would hinder him on his way. He is also careful not to grow too weak. In order to save time, he often eats while walking, with his mind always engaged elsewhere.

If he stops anywhere he knows that it is like being at an inn, where one must pay one's reckoning at the end of one's stay. If he finds some stream of spiritual nectar, he tastes some of it but he does not stop. Rather he hastens all the more to reach the sea. He avoids walking on mud. He slows down so as not to fall and get dirty. He avoids every opportunity to do evil. If he must walk in some dangerous place, he does so cautiously and quickly, trying to avoid danger as far as possible. If there is wind, hail or rain, then he hurries on his way. You, too, must draw closer to God in adverse times.

You must not walk by night so as to avoid falling into some precipice without Christ, as he says in John, VIII:[13] "You cannot approach God by the light of this world." If, through your own frailty or blindness, you were to fall into some error while walking, then you must stand up at once like a true pilgrim. You must not say to yourself: "I will go to confession at Easter." The longer one stays in the mud, the filthier one gets; the deeper one sinks into it, the harder it will be to stand up. There are confessors who will help you to get back on your feet.

When you are up again, you must run harder than before to make up for lost time and to catch up with your companions who have gone ahead. One must erase everything from one's mind, scorn this vile world, pay no attention to it, and consider it worthless. One must remember that these are nothing but shadows. Stop loving them and direct your love to the true things in our fatherland, in which our Father, who created us, dwells. That is the place from which we come, that is where we find real treasures, pleasures, glory, relatives, and friends.

Also Anaxagoras realized that this world is not our real fatherland. He was himself a pilgrim in an alien land. Once someone accused him of being indifferent to his own country. Raising his finger up to heaven and pointing to our real country, Anaxagoras answered: "On the contrary, my country lies very close to my heart and I love it very much. As far as I can, my heart and thoughts are always there."[14] When someone asked Socrates from which country he came, he pointed to heaven and answered: "From that one."[15]

PILGRIM SOUL: Through their faith, the Fathers in the Old Testament could see their celestial country from a distance, as Paul wrote to the Hebrews in [Ch.] II.[16] Yet their love made them hasten toward it. On the other hand, we are close, yet we are very indifferent. Heaven was closed to them. It is open to us, yet we do not move to reach it.

GUARDIAN ANGEL: We are all the guiltier for that.

PILGRIM SOUL: I am very weak. I do not see how I can persevere in my intent.

GUARDIAN ANGEL: It will be enough for you to be strong for the love of God. One cannot arrive there by one's strength and vigour; one must do it through love.

PILGRIM SOUL: I am already old and close to death. I cannot go very far.

GUARDIAN ANGEL: That is all the more reason for you to hasten your steps in order to get there before night falls and the gates close. You must forsake yourself through love so that your spirit may follow Christ more freely. God's grace may bestow some gift on you; yet you must not rest until you have reached him. You will have to render a full account of all that you have done. Therefore make sure that you avail yourself of every possible means on your way and that you use it well.

If you find someone along the road who has stopped or is going back or has fallen into a precipice, help him to get back on his feet and to resume his way. Do not abandon him. Try and encourage everyone to rise to God. Do all that you can to be the first one. Give up all worldly things in order to be lighter and faster. Render unto Caesar what is Caesar's and unto God what is God's.[17] Forsake your own self, too, and direct your heart, mind and all that you have toward your true fatherland. Do not be a coward, but persevere right up to the end with a brave heart. You will always be happy in this life, if for no other reason, because of your living unfailing hope of salvation. But you will be even more glorious in the life to come, when you will see all the heavens rejoice and be jubilant at your happiness.

There you will rest and see an end of your labours; there all your yearnings and desires will be brought to fruition and come to an end; there you will live happily without the cares, worries, anxiety, sorrow, annoyances, fears, and misery of this life; there you will be certain that you can sin no more, and you will live forever in divine grace; there, free from care, you will be satiated by God, yet not so satiated that you will become tepid; rather, you will forever be fervent in your love. Then you will reap the fruits of your labour, or rather of Christ's labour; then you will feel happy that you have suffered for God's love. Therefore, do not hesitate to go on your way as fervently as you can. I will always be with you, I will show you the way and I will help you to walk. Do not resist divine inspiration. If Christ calls you from heaven, hasten your steps and answer him. Remember that for your sake he was a pilgrim in this life for thirty-three years. Do not feel sorry that you have some walking to do now.

PILGRIM SOUL: Now I have realized that this life is an exile or rather hell and that heaven is my fatherland. I will not waste any more time, but I will make my way to heaven. You, angel, will accompany me. Farewell world! I am going to God and I leave you with all your wealth, honours, and dignities, or better, with all your worries, shame and poverty. I am leaving all my friends and

VII

DIALOGUE ABOUT THE DIVINE PROFESSION OF FAITH[1]

Characters: a Man and a Woman

MAN: For the honour and glory of God, I greatly desire the salvation of your soul and its supreme happiness.

WOMAN: You know full well that my soul is in your hands.

MAN: I would rather it were in God's hands.

WOMAN: Tell me what to do and I will not fail to do it.

MAN: I should like you to be in religion.

WOMAN: I do not think I should like to do that, for several reasons.

MAN: What if I pointed out to you an order after your own heart?

WOMAN: Perhaps I might join it, but so far I have not found any that I altogether like.

MAN: I know one that would certainly suit you and you would like if you heard about it.

WOMAN: That might be so, but I find it hard to believe.

MAN: This order is so perfect that it is all divine.

WOMAN: In that case it is not for me.

MAN: On the contrary, it is, because we must all seek perfection. In this order you must not change your domicile, but your ways; you must change your life, not your clothes; you must cut off all your evil thoughts and desires, not your hair; you must pray to God with your heart, not just with your lips; you must obey God's commands, not those of other people; you must be chaste in your heart and mind, avoid loving any earthly things and keep company with all the virtues.

71

WOMAN: I certainly wish that I could become perfect; yet I should not like to have to work too hard for it.

MAN: Then this is the way for you to do it. There is no easier and more perfect order in the world than this one.

WOMAN: It seems to me that to commit oneself to a deadly sin is tantamount to exposing oneself to a great danger.[2]

MAN: On the contrary, there is no safer way to reach God than this one.

WOMAN: Perhaps if you tell me enough about it I might be persuaded to join it. What is the name of this order?

MAN: Divine.

WOMAN: It could not have a worthier name.

MAN: Nor could the life of those belonging to it be a worthier one.

WOMAN: If you tell me more about it, perhaps I will join it.

MAN: There are no novices in this order: you take your vows immediately. That is not bad, since you do not have to commit yourself to anything dangerous.

WOMAN: I will let you decide. I know that in the end I shall do whatever you advise me to do.

MAN: I exhort you to join it and to take your vows immediately. You will feel more firmly rooted in goodness. Your works will be more pleasing to God.

WOMAN: Think it over carefully! One can take such steps only once. One must give them a lot of serious thought. If you decide that is the best course for me, I will not fail to do what you suggest.

MAN: In this order you can obtain a lot without danger. No one can join it except gentle spirits. I fully exhort you to form part of it.

WOMAN: Enough of all this talking! I will do as you wish.

MAN: Now I want you to make your profession of faith. I wish to be quite sure. Therefore I should like you to write it down with your own hand, or better with your heart. That way it will be more lasting and it will not be tepid.

WOMAN: I will write down in my heart all that you tell me. Let us begin in the name of Jesus Christ.

MAN: Your Grace has ascended in your mind to heaven, before the throne of the almighty Trinity, at Christ's feet, in the presence of the Virgin Mary and all the saints. Feeling faint at the thought of your own nothingness,[3] joined to God by faith, hope, and charity, you will say the following or similar words with all your heart:

TESTAMENT

"Be it known and clear to whoever will read this document that I, C.D. of C.,[4] sound of mind by divine grace and heavenly illumination, have realized on the one hand how great God's goodness is and how much love he bears me; on the other how wicked the world is and how many faults I am burdened with. Therefore I have decided to turn to God with all my love. Now, forever, and for all my life, I know through faith and I believe with my heart, soul, and mind, with all my might and strength, with my life, works, words and in every other possible way that there is only one God and three Persons. I believe God to be supremely simple, pure, eternal, immense, necessary, immutable, and almighty. I believe that in him there are infinite beauty, wisdom, justice, mercy, goodness, mildness, truth, charity, and every other attribute that can be supremely perfect. I believe that God newly created everything out of nothing. I believe that he takes care of all things with the highest providence, preserving, sustaining, and governing everything in the best possible way, with the highest goodness, wisdom, justice, mercy, and charity. I believe that there can be no error or shortcoming in his works and that he achieves everything perfectly. I believe that he foresees everything eternally and unfailingly with clear, certain, infallible knowledge. I believe that he loves us with eternal, endless, infinite, gratuitous, certain, fatherly, most pure, simple, divine love.

I also believe that out of excessive charity, for our salvation the Eternal Father caused his only Son to become a man. He was conceived by the Holy Spirit and born of the Virgin Mary. He lived and died on the Cross for us all. He descended to Limbo to free the holy Fathers. He rose again on the third day and ascended to heaven, where he sits at the right of the Father. I believe that he sent the Holy Spirit to inspire the Apostles. I believe in his teachings and I am certain by faith that his grace never fails. I believe that the lives of the saints and the Church of Christ are immaculate and holy. Finally, I believe all the things which I am bound to believe.

If through my own sinfulness, frailty, or ignorance, I have failed to do something or I have made some mistake, now and forever I confess my guilt and I repent. It is my intent to believe[5] only what is true, that is all I seek and believe in. I also wish to remove every obstacle to the rays of true faith and to believe with a supremely perfect act of faith, now, forever and in every minute of my life, especially at the point of death. I will believe in every instant for an infinite length of time, even if I were to live forever. If I were to lack faith, to err, to doubt, to hesitate or to waver, now I already declare and assure everyone that I will believe nothing except what is prescribed by the holy Church of Christ with all the stability and certainty of which I am capable.

Now and forever I offer myself to the Holy Trinity, ready and willing to expose myself to any sort of martyrdom possible in this life, an infinite number of times. So that my declaration may please God, now and forever I will accept this faith, which is supremely dear to me, with all my heart and will. I agree with all my power that it should dwell within me, and I am ever disposed to do all that I can think of to render it perfect. I intend to cherish it forever in my heart with an intense act of love accompanied by all the merits of our Lord. I intend to foster it within myself perfectly alive, operative, loving, fervent, and supremely perfect.

I have seen by experience the instability, infirmity, weakness and nothingness which exist in me as well as in other creatures. Unable to have any trust in myself and having lost confidence in all creatures, I will place all my hope in God alone. Now and forever I intend to depend on him alone and to place my hope in him alone. I intend to expect and acknowledge all good as deriving from divine goodness through Christ's merits. Now and forever I realize that I have done, do or can do nothing. I have known and loved, know and love, shall know and will nothing. I had, have or shall have no power whatsoever. I desire nothing. I have or shall have nothing. I am nothing. Therefore I have lost all hope and confidence in myself. With an intense act of hope, I will hope only in God's goodness, now and forever and in every instant.

If through my own sinfulness, frailty, or ignorance, I were ever to despair or to lose my trust in God; if I failed to recognize that all good derives from him and all evil from me; if as a result I were to grow proud of my own works and failed to give God all his honour, praise, and glory; now and forever I declare to God and to all creatures that in such a case I would be foolish, blind, and beside myself. I will never let my reason give its consent to such insane thoughts and ideas. Rather I will repeal, revoke, cancel and annul everything. I intend always to hope in God's divine goodness, with an intense act of hope and with all my heart. I wish never to abandon him and with clear understanding to recognize that all good comes from him and all evil from myself. I wish to offer supreme gratitude, honour, and glory to him alone and to consider myself nothing.

If I ever happened to be praised by someone, now and ever after I wish people to praise me not for my own works, but for those of God. Therefore I intend not to appropriate any praises with a sacrilegious mind, but to ascribe them all to God and to remain in my own misery. Depriving myself of all merits and ascribing all to God, I will remain in my own poverty.

I declare and promise forever to follow poverty, that is, to recognize forever that I own nothing. Divested of every merit and virtue, I will forever hide in Christ's side[6] and I intend never to leave it, placing all my hopes in him. Upon my death, I do not intend to appear before the lofty throne of the Trinity other than besmeared with the blood of Christ and enriched by his merits. I will not enter paradise in any other way or by any other means. If my frenzied, confused mind led me for some time to think that there is any good in me; if I placed any trust in my own works and merits; I declare to all faithful souls, to the angels, to the Virgin Mary, to Christ and to the Trinity that it is not my will and that in such case I err and deceive myself. Even now I take it all back, I repent and I place all my hope in God.

Even if I were to live forever, always and in every instant, while eating or drinking, at all times and in every place, I intend to hope only in God with an intense act of hope, helped by all the merits of the saints and of Christ and wholly pleasing to the lofty Trinity. Since I know that God alone is good and worthy of my love, I will forever give him my love, never loving anyone but him. He is supreme goodness and he loves me with infinite love. Therefore I realize that it would befit him and it would be my duty to give him infinite love, that is, to love him with continual, eternal, infinite, gratuitous, sincere love, just as he loves me. Yet I am unable to give him such intense love. Therefore I will now and ever elicit[7] from my heart an act of love toward him as intense, sincere and pure as I can, only in his honour. I intend to continue to offer him such love and infinitely to increase it, if possible. Since my love is imperfect, I intend that it should always be accompanied by every possible merit, especially the merits of Christ. Annihilated in myself and transformed into Christ, I intend always to love God with the same love with which he is loved by Christ's soul and to do so forever.

Through love I intend to become one in my heart with[8] the three Divine Persons, to forsake myself, and to abandon all creatures and to live for God alone. I will annihilate myself and become absorbed in God, so that I may love him, having become all divine. I intend to love him with infinite, eternal, continual, gratuitous, supreme love. At all times and in all places, even when eating or sleeping, I wish to breathe forth nothing but love, just as the Father and Son always spirate the Holy Spirit. If I ever happened to love a creature for some time, I do not want my love to dwell on it but to return to God in the end. If I failed to love him intensely for any period of time, even now I repent and ask to be forgiven. I wish everyone to understand that I intend always to persevere. Even now and ever I will love him with all my heart, with all my spirit, with all my mind and with all my power and energy. I intend my will to be fixed and steadfast on that point.

I will also acknowledge every good as coming from him. I will perceive his supreme goodness, infinite power, wisdom, charity, mercy, beauty, justice and other gifts in all his works. I will always think he is perfect in whatever he does. I will never cease to give him deep thanks with my heart, my works, my life, my words and in every other way possible to me. I will always praise him, exalt him, magnify him, and glorify him. I always intend to bless him, extol him, and honour him as far as possible. I intend to concentrate my thoughts on him always and forever, being inspired by him with excellent ideas.[9] I will never think about any creature except as it relates to divine love.

I will mortify myself and all the powers of my soul in this world, so that they will be alive only to God.

My heart, mind and all my being will grow completely estranged from creation and from the world. I will refuse to see, hear, understand, or know the world unless I can use it in honour of God. I want God always to be my ultimate aim. I want everything to relate to him; I want all my wishes to end in him, I want all the course of my life to lead to him. I want all my works to be prompted by a simple, sincere, right intention. I want to seek divine honour in everything. This is to be my aim forever, every second of my life. Therefore I will even sleep, eat and do everything else to live for God and to serve him.

For his honour and glory I also want to induce my fellowbeings to do good and to draw them to God as much as possible with my words, prayers, example, and life. I will fulfil the duty of charity by enlightening, advising, correcting, tolerating, and comforting everyone. I will pray for them, forgive them and do as much good to them as possible. I intend, resolve and want to provide for everyone's temporal, bodily, and spiritual needs.

Even if I possessed infinite treasures, pleasures, delights, and glory; even if I could enjoy infinite paradises;[10] I will give them all up and descend into infinite hells if it is for the glory of God. Even if I had supreme beauty and power, the gift of supreme eloquence, the approval and favour of all the people in the world; even if I were intensely loved, honoured, and revered by everyone; even if everyone considered me a saint and I knew all there is to know about creation; even if I could know, understand and taste divine mysteries, foresee all future events, and remember all past ones; even if I knew all the secrets of the human heart and all the divine secrets and I had all that man can desire; even now and ever I resolve to deprive myself of all if it is in God's honour. I would rather be forever blind and mute, ignorant, stupid, and devoid of reason. I would rather be considered evil, hated and rejected by all. I would prefer to be disgusting to everyone, barren, and insipid, persecuted by all. Finally, I would prefer to be forever in all imaginable misery.

I propose, intend, and promise now and ever, in every instant, never to offend the divine majesty any more. I am grievously sorry for all my faults, or better, for all the wrongs committed by all creatures against God, my Lord. Now and ever, whether I remember or not, in every instant, I bitterly repent only for the honour of his divine majesty. I am deeply sorry that I am not sorry enough, because I should be capable of infinite sorrow, or better, infinite sorrows as would suit my numberless sins. In order to experience supreme sorrow, I want to become transformed into Christ. If I had had an opportunity, a suitable place, a chance, a way and an occasion, without divine grace I would have committed infinite sins, had I lived for an infinite length of time. Therefore I am taking them all upon myself and I am bitterly sorry for them all. In order to do due penance, by an express act of my will I resolve to endure every punishment the Lord will see fit to send me in this life, or even all the punishments that could be sent to a being while it is alive. Since that would not be satisfaction enough, even now I resolve and accept all the punishments of Purgatory. Since those are not enough, being in God's glory, I accept not only every possible martyrdom, punishment, infamy, exile, imprisonment, persecution, cross, death, and annihilation. I also accept all the pains of hell and of infinite hells, so long as I can endure them. Since all these punishments together are not enough to atone for my sins, annihilated in myself and transformed into Christ, I will suffer all that he suffered for thirty-three years. Since not even that would be enough, I commit myself to the merciful arms of Christ on the cross. Only through him do I expect to obtain forgiveness for my sins.

Now and ever I also exult and rejoice in all the good God has worked through me and will work in the future: all the good works, merits, and virtues of those who are now alive and of those who will be alive, even if the world were to last for an infinite length of time; all the virtues, merits, and glory of all the angels and saints in paradise; the virtue of the Virgin Mary and her happiness and glory; all the merits of Christ, his triumph, and victory, and all his blessedness. I rejoice in all divine perfection and in the infinite glory and happiness of the three Divine Persons.

Now and ever and in every instant I will seek to experience perfect bliss. I wish it could be infinite and I wish I could perennially experience it and never be without it. I promise to do so forever and in every instant of my life. I also intend and resolve now and forever to avoid every opportunity to do evil and to seek every opportunity to do good. I also forgive every affront which I may have received, only for the pure love of Christ. I resolve, decide, and promise that I will forgive everything even now, forever, and in every instant, even if I were to live indefinitely and I were to receive an infinite number of insults from an infinite number of people, against all fairness and justice. I intend to forgive everything for every second of time. Transformed into Christ, I will forgive everyone; better, I will love them deeply. For their sake I am disposed to suffer, shed my own blood, and undergo a thousand deaths[11] with Christ. Transformed into Christ, I pray with Christ and I ask my Father to forgive them.

I profess and take a solemn public vow, promising poverty, obedience, and chastity. First of all I promise always to live in poverty, that is, without feeling any love for creation. I promise always to be aware, with true understanding, that I own nothing, I have no power, I have no will, I have no knowledge, and I can achieve nothing.

I also promise God perfect obedience in always carrying out all divine inspirations with all my power and in never being unwilling to do so. I resolve to do so now and forever.

I also promise God perfect chastity. I will always seek to have an immaculate heart and mind. I will never think about, desire, yield to, or want anything which may displease God. Even more, I will never sully my mind thinking of any creature or loving it. Rather I will always remain united to God and absorbed in him.

So I promise to serve my Lord with immaculate purity and also to draw into his service all the ladies-in-waiting who serve in my house, that is, all the powers of my soul.[12] Spurning the world,[13] I will choose the one who created me as my one and only father, his Son who redeemed me as my brother and the Holy Spirit as my bridegroom, giving him all my love as a dowry. I promise him not to want anything except what pleases him at all times and in every place.

Since I cannot achieve anything without God, now and forever I beg him to grant me that I may carry out all I have promised and all that I am disposed to do with all my heart. Now and forever and in every instant I commend to him all those who stand in need, as charity prescribes and requires. Since I do not wish to offend God, I will not commit myself to incurring any mortal sin in any promise which I have made or shall make. The same applies to all the vows I have pronounced. I only intend to be bound to anything mortal to the extent that God has bound me.

I resolve to do now all the above things and all that can be done in God's honour, as far as it lies within my power. I determine so to directly will, so to act, and to undergo everything with a pure intention now and ever, in every instant even if I were to live forever. I will do so with steadfast intention, will, habit, faith, union, and grace. I will be annihilated and transformed into Christ so as to participate in his merits as much as possible. I will be totally absorbed in God for eternity. I will have no one but him.

If I ever happened to have second thoughts, break my faith or fail in my profession of faith, even now I declare to God and to all the world that it is not my intention to fail or to take back what I have promised. Therefore I cancel and annul everything and I beg God to consider it as if not done.

I want this to be my last will and all my wishes will come to an end. I promise always to hold this as ratified and confirmed. I confess now, before I reach the point of death, and forever, that I am a great sinner, that I have placed all my hope in God and that I do not hope to save myself except through Christ. In witness thereof I call upon the lofty Trinity, the Virgin Mary, all the saints and all creatures, even also my own conscience. In proof of which I D.d.C.[14] have written the present document with my own hand. 1539."[15]

Printed in Venice

by
Nicolò d'Aristotile called il Zoppino

in the year 1542.

NOTES

Biblical quotations are taken from Bibliorum Sacrorum iuxta Clementinam Nova Editio Breviario Perpetuo et Concordantiis Aucta Adnotatis etiam Locis qui in Monumentis Fidei Sollemnioribus et in Liturgia Romana usurpari consueverunt, ed. Aloisius Gramatica (Vatican City: Typis Polyglottis Vaticanis, 1959). All quotations refer to this edition because the text incorporates the Vulgate, which was the Bible in most use during Ochino's time.

Dialogue 1

1. *innamorarsi di Dio* in the original.
2. No explicit statement to this effect appears in St. Matthew, 20.
3. Pliny the Elder mentions the salamander in his *Natural History* X as being able to put out a fire. The belief was carried over into the medieval bestiaries, so that the salamander came to symbolize the spirit of fire because of its supposed capacity to survive in the middle of flames.
4. Matthew, 19:17.
5. *ombratica* in the original.
6. See Aristotle, *The Nicomachean Ethics*, ed. and trans. H. Rackham (London-Cambridge,Mass.: Heinemann, 1968), II.vi.12-17, for the idea that moral virtue consists in a mean.
7. Romans 8:35.
8. This somewhat puzzling remark may perhaps be partly explained by reference to St. Augustine, for whom God does not only mean the Father, as *ho theos* did for the ancient Greeks, but the whole Godhead, the basic divinity unfolding itself into three Persons, the Father, the Son and the Holy Spirit. Thus the supreme goodness of the Godhead as a whole could be loved by the three Persons; see E. J. Fortman, *The Triune God. A Historical Study of the Doctrine of the Trinity* (Philadelphia: Westminster, 1972), 141.
9. For the distinction between different types of love, see St. Thomas Aquinas, *Summa Theologiae*, ed. P. Caramello (Turin: Marietti, 1952-56), vol. 1, Ia IIae, Question XXVI, Art. 1.

10. Ochino's remarks relate to traditional belief, according to which angels were endowed with free will when they were created, and erred because of their pride. The role of angels as messengers of God is a traditional one. See "Anges," in *Dictionnaire de spiritualité ascétique et mystique*, ed. M. Viller, S.J. (Paris: Gabriel Beauchesne et ses Fils, 1937), vol. 1, cols. 583 et seq.; see also Dialogue 6, note 2.

11. Matthew, 6:24.

12. See W. J. Courtenay, "Nominalism and Late Medieval Religion," in C. Trinkaus and H. A. Oberman, eds., in *The Pursuit of Holiness in Late Medieval and Renaissance Religion* (Leiden: Brill, 1974), 57: "Ockhamist epistemology is not simply empirical; it is based on visual experience, and it takes the eye as the primary sense organ around which to build a theory of knowledge."

13. *volontà* is feminine in Italian, while *intelletto* is masculine. The masculine and feminine genders have been preserved in the translation in order to convey the image of a queen and her minister. The same applies to the third dialogue.

14. The Duchess's remarks relate to the medieval controversy about whether love or knowledge was the best means to approach God. Being a Franciscan, Ochino stresses the part played by love, though he also follows St. Thomas Aquinas in admitting the importance of the intellect. See Aquinas, *Summa*, vol. 1, Ia IIae, Question XXVII, Art. 2, for the author's confutation of Pseudo-Dionysius' emphasis on love as opposed to knowledge. The attribution of love to the seraphim and of knowledge to the cherubim derives from Pseudo-Dionysius. See *De Caelesti Hierarchia*, ed. P. Hendrix (Leiden: Brill, 1959), VII.i.15.

15. The distinction between the procession of the intellect resulting in the Word and the procession of love resulting in the Holy Spirit is derived from St. Thomas Aquinas. See Fortnam, *Triune God*, 206.

16. Corinthians I, 13:12, and Romans, 1:18-20.

17. See St. Bonaventure, "The Journey of the Mind to God," in *The Works of St. Bonaventure*, trans. J. de Vinck (Paterson, N.J.: St. Anthony Guild Press, 1960), vol. 1, 45, for a similar image.

18. This quotation appears to be a combination of the following:
    a) Timothy I, 6:16: ". . . *qui solus habet immortalitatem et lucem inhabitat inaccessibilem . . .*"; b) Psalm 103:02: ". . . *amictus lumine sicut vestimento . . .*"; c) Psalm 17:12: "*Et posuit tenebras latibulum suum . . . .*"

19. See note 8.

20. Corinthians I, 13:9.

21. In his remarks about memory and will as the two operative principles in the procession of the Trinity, Ochino may have been influenced by the thought of Duns Scotus. See Fortman, *Triune God*, 221.

22. To spirate is a theological term meaning to breathe or generate. It is used to express the creative function of the Deity conceived as the action of breathing.

23. See Fortman, *Triune God*, 144, for the following comment about St. Augustine's trinitarian doctrine: "Thus . . . the three Persons are three subjects of one divine activity who are not accidentally nor substantially but relationally distinct, or three relationally distinct subsistents in one intellectual divine nature."

24. It was one of St. Augustine's major concerns to reconcile man's freedom in relation to contingent acts with the foreknowledge which God necessarily possesses. He concluded that the human will is free, but that grace is indispensable as a basis of merit. For St. Thomas man is free in respect of finite goods, but determined in respect of infinite good. Divine will does not annul man's free will. See "Liberté," in *Dictionnaire de Théologie Catholique contenant l'Exposé des Doctrines de la Théologie Catholique, leurs Preuves et leur Histoire*, ed. A. Vacant and E. Mangenot (Paris: Letouzey et Ané, 1926), vol. 9, part 1, cols. 671 et seq. For an example of the attitude toward the same problem on the part of a fifteenth-century thinker, see H. A. Oberman, *The Harvest of Medieval Theology. Gabriel Biel and Late Medieval Nominalism* (Cambridge, Mass.: Harvard University Press, 1963), particularly 185-90; Biel interprets predestination as God's foreknowledge of man's future behaviour. Yet God has decreed that no one will be damned unless for personal guilt and that acceptation will require personal merits. The Duchess's emphasis on the importance of free will at

a time when discussions about predestination were inspired by the impact of Protestant thought could be an attempt on Ochino's part to emphasize her orthodoxy, as well as his own.

25. The remark derives from Beato Egidio, one of St. Francis' earliest followers. See E. Gilson, *The Philosophy of St. Bonaventure* (Paterson, N.J.: St. Anthony Guild Press, 1965), 72.

26. Romans, 1:21. Also St. Bonaventure often expressed his aversion to idle knowledge. See, for instance, "The Triple Way or Love Enkindled," in *Works*, vol. 1, 65-66.

27. Ezechiel, 28:3. In reality, the character mentioned in the Bible is the King of Tyre.

28. No such statement appears in St. Matthew, Ch. 3. Ochino's remark probably refers to the sermon on the mount in Ch.5.

29. This may be an extremely free rendering of Psalm 72, in which the wickedness of those who question God's wisdom is decried. See particularly line 22: ". . . *et ego ad nihilum redactus sum et nescivi, ut iumentum factus sum apud te.*" The mention of Christ's sacred stigmata appears to be Ochino's own addition.

30. Titus, 3:9.

31. The letters N. I. Ch., that is, *Nostro Iesu Christo*, appear at the end of this paragraph.

32. Romans, 1:20. See also St. Bonaventure, "Journey," 15-16.

33. The mention of an infinite number of worlds, appearing also in the second and third dialogues, is perhaps due to the influence of nominalism, according to which our world is contingent, not an ontologically necessary outflow or reflection of eternal structures of being, but the result of a decree, a contract, a *pactum Dei*. Thus the possibility of the creation of an infinite number of worlds is always potentially present; see H. A. Oberman, "The Shape of Late Medieval Thought: the Birthpangs of the Modern Era," in C. Trinkaus and H. A. Oberman, eds., *Pursuit of Holiness*, 12: ". . . the nominalist point of departure is that God could have decreed — *de potentia absoluta* — to create another world, to choose other means of salvation, and to establish another order."

34. The source of this quotation remains obscure. Fire is generally associated with God's wrath in the Old Testament. Fire as a metaphor of love appears somewhat later. On the other hand, the idea of meditation as a means of understanding God often

appears in the Psalms. Thus this passage may have been partly inspired by Psalm 13: *"Et meditabor in omnibus operibus tuis,"* or by Psalm 142:5: *"Meditatus sum in omnibus operibus tuis,"* with its final emphasis on divine goodness.

35. See St. Bonaventure, "Letter Containing Twenty-five Points to Remember," in *Works,* vol. 3, 256 for a similar suggestion which, however, is limited to someone in holy orders. Ochino does not make such a specification.

36. John, 10:9.

37. *anima* is treated as a feminine in English in order to preserve the image of the soul being a sister to the body.

38. *nell'armario della sua memoria* in the original.

39. This appears to be a somewhat free version of Romans, 8:32: *"Qui etiam Filio suo non pepercit, sed pro nobis omnibus tradidit illum, quomodo non etiam cum illo omnia nobis donabit?".*

40. *curiose* in the original.

41. Psalm 33:9.

42. The Duchess's new proposal on how to approach God, which contradicts her previous one, brings her close to the mysticism of the Spanish *dejados,* a group that had some influence on Juan de Valdés. See D. de Sta. Teresa, *Juan de Valdés 1498(?)-1541* (Rome: Gregorian University, 1957), 32: "El alma no tiene que hacer nada; presentar a Dios la postura de no querer hacer nada ante su iniciativa; "dejarse" en una palabra; el amor divino le enseñaria lo que ha de hacer." Valdés, however, does not reject the role of the intellect in the search for God; he only rejects idle speculation. An example may be found in his *Considerazione 12,* quoted by ibid., 159: ". . . così la ragione, che è nell'uomo interiore, è abile a conoscer Dio non per se stessa, ma col medesimo Dio, e similmente tutte le cose che manifesta Dio . . . Ora essendo ciò vero, intendiamo che Dio ha posto nell'uomo la ragione a fine che con essa conosca Dio, ma con Dio e non per suoi discorsi." Ochino's conclusion with regard to the role of reason in the first dialogue resembles that of Juan de Valdés.

43. See Pseudo-Dionysius, *De Caelesti Hierarchia,* VII.i.15-16, for a description of the seraphim and the cherubim and VII.iii.18, for the illumination of the intellect.

44. Hebrews, 5:12-14.

Notes

45. Acts, 2:3.
46. Luke, 24:32.
47. Hebrews, not 10, but 4:12. Ochino's rendering is somewhat free.
48. Luke, 12:49.
49. Exodus, 3:2 et seq.; Kings IV, 2:11; Acts, 2:3. Most of this final passage derives from Baldassarre Castiglione. See *Il Cortegiano*, ed. S. Del Missier (Novara: De Agostini, 1968), bk. 4, 573: ". . . cumulando insieme tutte le bellezze farà un concetto universale e ridurrà la moltitudine d'esse alla unità di quella sola che generalmente sopra la umana natura si spande," and 578: ". . . questo è lo ardente rubo di Mosè, le lingue dispartite di foco, l'infiammato carro di Elia, il quale raddoppia la grazia e felicità nell'anime di coloro che son degni di vederlo . . . ."

Dialogue 2

1. Luke, 17:21.
2. See Dialogue 1, note 33.
3. See St. Bonaventure, "Triple Way," 77, for the idea that nothing below God can please the human soul, and " Journey," 28 et seq., for the resemblance between the soul and the Trinity.
4. The Crates mentioned here is probably Crates of Thebes, Zeno's teacher, who flourished c. 326 B.C. See Diogenes Laertius, *Lives of Eminent Philosophers*, trans. R. D. Hicks (London-Cambridge, Mass.: Heinemann, 1959), vol. 2, 88-97. Crates' simple life style was inspired by Diogenes, the Cynic philosopher who was his teacher. According to Plutarch, Crates asserted that luxury and extravagance are the causes of civil discord. See "Advice about Keeping Well," in *Moralia*, trans. F. C. Babbit (London-Cambridge, Mass.: Heinemann, 1962), vol. 2, 235.
5. Numerous remarks about the insatiability of human desires appear in Seneca's works. See *De Beneficiis*, trans. S. Guglielmino (Bologna: Zanichelli, 1967), 424-25: "*Quid interest, quot eripuerit regna, quot dederit, quantum terrarum tributo premat? Tantum illi deest, quantum cupit.*" Seneca is alluding to Alexander the Great. Ochino may have been quoting from this work.

6. This remark may have been inspired by Plato. See *The Laws*, trans. R. G. Bury (London-Cambridge, Mass.: Heinemann, 1967), bk. 4, 716D, 297: ". . . to engage in sacrifice and communion with the gods continually, by prayers and offerings and devotions of every kind, is a thing most noble and good and helpful towards the happy life . . ."; see also Plutarch's remarks about Plato in "On the Delays of the Divine Vengeance," in *Moralia*, vol. 7, 195.

7. The gymnosophists were members of an ancient Hindu sect of ascetics who despised the world and lived in contact with nature. They are mentioned, among others, by Plutarch, "On the Fortune or the Virtue of Alexander," in *Moralia*, vol. 4, 413-15.

8. Cleanthes of Assos (331-232 B.C.) was Zeno's pupil and succeeded his teacher as leader of the Stoics. See Diogenes Laertius, *Lives*, vol. 2, 272-85. Allusions to the importance Cleanthes ascribed to the strength of mind of the wise man may be found in Diogenes Laertius' biography of Zeno in ibid., 230-33; See also E. Zeller, *The Stoics, Epicureans and Sceptics*, trans. and ed. O. J. Reichel (New York: Russell and Russell, 1962), ch. 10, 257, for Cleanthes' concept of strength of mind as the common root of all virtues.

9. This appears as a stanza in *ottava rima* in the original.

Dialogue 3

1. According to Ptolemy, who flourished c. 140 A.D., the First Mover was the outermost motionless sphere which imparted motion to the entire system of eight rotating heavens at the centre of which was the earth. The First Mover had already been identified with God by Aristotle. See *Metaphysics*, trans. H. Tredennick (London-Cambridge, Mass.: Heinemann, 1969), XII.vii.1-9.144-51. St. Thomas Aquinas followed Aristotle and used an argument from motion as one of his proofs for the existence of God. See *Summa*, vol. 1, Ia, Question II, Art. 3.

2. The thought appears in various works by Aristotle, for instance, *Nicomachean Ethics*, III.ii.3-4.

3. See Dialogue 2, note 8.

4. See Dialogue 2, note 6.

5. *non si impaccia del mondo* in the original.

6. Theologians distinguish between the generation or procession of the Trinity, which is internal, and the creative process, which is external. The Father created the world only after he had generated the Word. Thus the Trinity existed before anything else did. See Fortman, *Triune God*, 91, on this point in relation to St. John of Damascus.

7. See Dialogue 1, note 13.

8. See Aquinas, *Summa*, vol. 1, Ia, Question LXXXII, Art. 4, for the roles played by the intellect and the will.

9. *per lume naturale* in the original.

10. *per lume acquisito o per infuso et sopranaturale* in the original.

11. Aquinas, *Summa*, vol. 2, IIa IIae, Question CLXXXIV, Art. 3, distinguishes between counsels and precepts. The distinction does not appear as such in the Gospel. The first one to formulate it distinctly was St. Ambrose in his *De Viduis*. He identified precepts with the Law and counsels with Grace. According to St. Thomas Aquinas, Christian perfection is based on the precept to love God and our fellow-beings. In his view, counsels are the best way in which to place one's inner freedom in the service of perfect charity in that they help to carry out the required precepts. Counsels were included among the works of supererogation. See *Dictionnaire de spiritualité*, vol. 2, part 2, cols. 1594 et seq.

12. See Aquinas, *Summa*, vol. 1, Ia, Question LXXVIII, Arts. 1-4, for a description of the powers of the soul. Ochino's allegory of the powers of the soul belongs in the tradition of personification of abstract elements, an example of which may be found, for instance, in Boethius' personification of philosophy. See C. S. Lewis, "Allegory," in *The Allegory of Love* (New York: Oxford University Press, 1958), 2, 44: "Allegory, in some sense, belongs not to medieval man but to man, or even to mind, in general. It is of the very nature of thought and language to represent what is immaterial in picturable terms."

13. *sarebbe facil cosa che io ci rimanessi* in the original.

14. *che io mi intricassi ne li beneficii* in the original.

15. Perhaps significantly, Ochino does not appear to believe that priests or monks have any greater chance of obtaining salvation than a merchant.

Notes

16. *eccita se stessa trarre da Dio atti intensissimi di amore* in the original.
17. *havere uno essere divino* in the original.
18. *che hanno il core a casa del divino amore* in the original.
19. *ne rifermandoli, ne molto manco discendendo al basso* in the original.
20. *di balzo tutto il mandi a Dio* in the original.

Dialogue 4

1. *visto la figura* in the original. Ochino's fourth dialogue is based on Ubertino da Casale's *Arbor Vitae Crucifixae Jesu*. See R. Belladonna, "Bernardino Ochino's Fourth Dialogue (*Dialogo del Ladrone in Croce*) and Ubertino da Casale's *Arbor Vitae*: Adaptation and Ambiguity," *Bibliothèque d'Humanisme et Renaissance*, 47, no. 1, (1985), 125-45. See the accompanying notes for the numbers of the chapters, columns, and lines in the *Arbor Vitae* from which Ochino derived his most important borrowings; For Ochino's dwelling on the Passion in this dialogue, see E. Auerbach,"*Excursus. Gloria Passionis*," in *Literary Language and its Public in Late Latin Antiquity and in the Middle Ages*, trans. R. Manheim (New York: Pantheon Books, 1965), 67. The contemplation of Christ on the Cross is typical of Italian Evangelism. See Juan de Valdés, *Alfabeto Cristiano; Dialogo con Giulia Gonzaga*, ed. B. Croce (Bari: Gius. Laterza e figli, 1938), 71: "E sappiate certo che non è luogo nessuno dove meglio possiate conoscere Iddio che in Cristo crucifisso." See also Benedetto da Mantova, *Il Beneficio di Cristo con le versioni del sec. XVI. Documenti e testimonianze*, ed. S. Caponetto (Florence: Sansoni, 1972), 65: "E, perchè tutta la essenza della messa consiste in questo divinissimo sacramento, quando il cristiano vi si ritruova, doverebbe tenere sempre gli occhi della mente fissi nella passione di questo nostro benignissimo Signore, contemplando da un lato lui in croce, carico di tutti li peccati nostri, e da l'altro Dio, che li castiga, flagellando invece di noi il suo dilettissimo Figliuolo." The good thief appears also in this work on p. 35.
2. Matthew, 27:46.

3. There is no scriptural basis for the belief that Christ cast his shadow upon the good thief. For St. Peter curing the sick with his shadow, see Acts, 5:15.
4. *vero e divino solo* in the 1542 original. This differs from U. Rozzo's interpretation which reads *vero e divino sole*.
5. Ubertino da Casale, *Arbor Vitae Crucifixae Jesu*, ed. C. T. Davis (Turin: Bottega d'Erasmo, 1961), ch. 13, col. 2, line 2, 319.
6. ibid., col. 1, lines 4-6, 319.
7. Matthew, 27:44.
8. *s'apersero le finestre delli divini tesori* in the original. See St. Bonaventure, "The Tree of Life," in *Works*, vol. 1, 127-28 for the imagery in this part of the dialogue.
9. da Casale, *Arbor Vitae*, ch. 13, col. 2, lines 10-14 and 35-40, 319; ch. 14, col. 1, lines 32-38, 321.
10. Luke, 23:41; also, da Casale, *Arbor Vitae*, ch. 13, col. 2, lines 50-54 and 56-58, 319.
11. da Casale, *Arbor Vitae*, ch. 13, col. 1 line 58; col. 2, lines 1-17 and 13-19, 319-20.
12. ibid., lines 26-27, 320.
13. Luke, 23:43.
14. da Casale, *Arbor Vitae*, ch. 13, col. 1, lines 27-47, 320.
15. ibid., lines 49-51, 320.
16. ibid., ch. 14, col. 2, lines 17-42 and 49-54, 320.
17. ibid., col. 1, lines 1-2 and 26-28, 321.
18. Genesis, 4:1-16.
19. *ibid.*, 9:21-25.
20. *ibid.*, 16 et seq. The dichotomy presented by Isaac and Ishmael, already important in Jewish thought, is also mentioned by St. Paul in his Epistle to the Galatians, 4:22-31.
21. Genesis, 27.
22. The account of Christ's descent into Hell and His deliverance of the just and holy souls of the Patriarchs in Limbo derives from the apocryphal Gospels of Bartholomew and Nicodemus. The episode was of enormous importance as an iconographic source in the Middle Ages.
23. The Empyrean or heaven of fire was a late medieval addition to the system of concentric heavens created by classical and Arab astronomy. It was conceived as an all-embracing heaven of heavens, where God and the blessed spirits dwelt. It was

called fiery because of its splendour, which was symbolical of the light of God illuminating the angels and saints.

24. Matthew, 20:1-16.

25. *Il* [i.e. *al*] *primo Ladrone disse terra sei, et in terra tornerai; all'ultimo del Vecchio Testamento, hoggi sarai con meco in Paradiso* in the original. Though the text is slightly corrupt, the meaning is clarified by reference to the previously quoted parable. The first thief is identified with the labourers who were hired first, whereas the good thief is like the last hired labourers who got their full pay.

26. The woman is now identified as the Duchess of Camerino.

Dialogue 5

1. *voglio aspettare un puoco di bonaccia, e ch'el me facciun puoco di buono viso* in the original.

2. *ti facesse festa* in the original.

3. *tenir il pie in due staffe* in the original.

4. Because of its importance in navigation, the anchor had been a symbol of safety for centuries before the Christian era. In using it on funeral monuments, jewels, rings, etc., Christians gave the anchor the higher meaning of hope in future life. That is why in early Christian thought the anchor is associated with the monogram of Christ. The first scriptural use of this symbol is in the Epistle to the Hebrews, 6:19-20: "We have hope set before us as an anchor of the soul, sure and firm." Seldom used in medieval ornamentation, the anchor reappeared in the Baroque period, often associated with the patron saints of ports, seamen, etc. See *New Catholic Encyclopedia*, ed. W. J. McDonald et al. (New York: McGraw-Hill Book Co., 1967), vol. 1, 486.

5. *volsi già fare un salto* in the original.

6. Matthew, 22:21.

7. *non aspettar d'haver la testa sotto la mannaia* in the original.

Dialogue 6

1. The theme of the pilgrimage of human life already appears in the Old Testament in its three related aspects: a) departure,

symbolical of ascetic detachment from earthly things; b) earthly life as an exile from God; c) earthly life as a journey toward the heavenly Jerusalem. The first aspect appears, for instance, in Abraham's departure for Ur, Genesis, 12:1; the second may be found in Leviticus 19:34-36, in Job, and in the Psalms; the last may be found in Exodus and elsewhere. The themes reappear in the New Testament and were subsequently used by Christian writers, for instance, by St. Augustine, *Enarratio. in Ps.*, XXXVIII and elsewhere. See *Dictionnaire de spiritualité*, vol. 12, cols. 890 et seq.

2. In his interpretation of the fall of the angels Ochino may have been influenced by his readings of the early Church Fathers. Theological beliefs relating to angels developed only gradually. Their development was influenced by Pseudo-Enoch, a part of the Old Testament later discarded as apocryphal by St. Jerome. Two questions were the object of particularly intense debate in the early years of Christianity: a) whether angels were indeed pure spirit (according to Pseudo-Enoch some of them had united themselves to earthly women, giving origin to giants; they had also revealed their secrets to those women); b) whether angels were invariably good. The first question was finally settled by Pseudo-Dionysius, who affirmed the purely spiritual nature of angels; the second question was answered by St. Augustine, according to whom angels are immutably good and cannot therefore become demons. A related question was whether angels had been created before heaven and earth, as most Greek Fathers tended to believe, or whether they were a remnant of a previous world created before this world, as Origenes affirmed. The fall of a group of them, a belief originating from Pseudo-Enoch, was variously attributed to lust, envy, pride or negligence.

3. *fu comprensore* in the original.

4. Matthew, 19:21.

5. ibid., 6:19-21.

6. ibid., 10:37.

7. ibid., 5:29.

8. ibid., 5:30.

9. St. Bonaventure, "On the Perfection of Life Addressed to Sisters," in *Works*, vol. 1, ch. 6, para. 2, 239, for the image of the sinner hiding in Christ's side.

Notes

10. *non compra le gabelle degli impacci* in the original.
11. Philippians, 1:23.
12. *tre grani di miglio* in the original.
13. John, more appropriately 11:9-10.
14. This anecdote about Anaxagoras (500-428 B.C.) has been preserved by Diogenes Laertius, *Lives*, vol. 1, 137.
15. Plutarch, "On Exile," in *Moralia*, vol. 3, 529. In Plutarch's account, Socrates is not quoted as saying that he is a citizen of heaven, but a citizen of the world, a "Cosmian". See also Cicero, *Tusculan Disputations*, trans. J. E. King (London-Cambridge, Mass.: Heinemann, 1966), V.xxxvii.108.533-34, for the same anecdote; again, the word used by Cicero is *mundanus*.
16. Hebrews, in reality 11:1-3.
17. See Dialogue 5, note 6.

Dialogue 7

1. *divina professione* in the original.
2. The woman has misunderstood Ochino's remarks and fears that the rules of the order which he is suggesting that she should join will be too lax or even immoral.
3. *per humiltà tutta in se stessa mancando* in the original.
4. Caterina, Duchess of Camerino.
5. *l'intelletto mio ha da credere* in the 1540 text; *l'intento mio è di credere* in the 1542 text.
6. See Dialogue 6, note 9.
7. *elicere* in the 1540 text; *eleggere* in the 1542 text.
8. *farmi intima e cordiale alle tre divine persone* in the original.
9. *havendo di lui ottimi concetti* in the 1540 text; *havendo da lui ottimi concetti* in the 1542 text.
10. *infiniti paradisi* in the original.
11. The imitation of Christ, including the transformation of the sinner into Him, is basic in mystical literature. See S. Ozment, "The Spiritual Traditions," in *The Age of Reform (1250-1550): An Intellectual and Religious History of Late Medieval and Reformation Europe* (New Haven: Yale University Press, 1980), 117: "A final basic characteristic of mysticism is its extreme attachment to what I earlier described as the principle of 'likeness'. . . Being 'like' God (*similitudo, conformitas*) was, for all, the essential

condition of union with God . . . Hence, the repeated stress by all mystical writers on withdrawal from the world, transcending reason, and retreating into the depths of one's being where one is most 'like God'." The imitation of and transformation into Christ are basic themes in Italian Evangelism. See B. da Mantova, *Il Beneficio*, 54: "Da questa considerazione nasce l'altro modo del vestirsi di Cristo, il qual possiamo chiamar esemplare, perchè il cristiano dee regolare tutta la vita sua all'esempio di Cristo, conformandosi con lui in tutti i pensieri, le parole e le operazioni, lasciando la mala vita passata e vestendosi della nuova, cioè di quella di Cristo."

12. See Dialogue 3, note 12.

13. *dando de calci al mondo* in the original.

14 *Duchessa di Camerino*.

15. *a di iiij. di Settembre M.D.XXXVJ* in the 1540 text. The two colophons read as follows: *Stampata in Vinetia per Nicolò d'Aristotile detto il Zoppino. L'anno M.D.XXXXII.* for the 1542 text; *Stampato in Ast[i] per Francesco Garrone de Livorno et cittadino di Ast[i] nel Anno del nostro Signore M.D.XXXX a di vij Marzo* for the 1540 text. The Duchess's initials at the end of this spiritual testament appear as D.D.C. in the 1542 text. The signature in the 1540 text appears as Io. N.

Renaissance and Reformation Texts in Translation

The purpose of this series is to provide translations in modern prose and in modest format of important texts of the Reformation and Renaissance, with emphasis on texts illustrating some major aspect of thought, and especially humanism and the humanist strain in the Reformation.

1. Lorenzo Valla *'The Profession of the Religious' and the principal arguments from 'The Falsely-Believed and Forged Donation of Constantine'* translated by Olga Zorzi Pugliese
2. Giovanni Della Casa *Galateo* translated by Konrad Eisenbichler and Kenneth Bartlett
3. Bernardino Ochino *Seven Dialogues* translated by Rita Belladonna